Writing Tales
Level One
Teacher's Guide

It is with immense gratitude and praise to God that I dedicate this project to my family: my husband Glen and my children Kristen, Timothy and Melissa.

Introduction

<u>Writing Tales</u> was born out of my experience teaching a writing class to 3rd and 4th grade students in our classical co-op. A desire to teach writing from the classical approach led to a need to make the subject enjoyable, and before I knew it, <u>Writing Tales</u> was born.

The classical approach to teaching writing is based on the 12 ancient levels of instruction from the Greeks called the Progymnasmata. In a nutshell, the theory is that students best learn to write on their own by copying well-written models first. At the same time, they learn the mechanics of the English language by studying and analyzing these models. These books are based on the first level of the Progymnasmata, which has the students studying and re-writing fables and legends.

As I was teaching the first "draft" of this curriculum, I noticed a difference in how much the students enjoyed writing their stories based on how much creative liberty I would allow them to take. When I required them to strictly re-tell the original story in their own words without any creative touches whatsoever, there was a definite lack of joy and pride in the finished product. On the other hand, when I allowed the students to be creative and add their own ideas to the original story, they loved writing! Therefore, I have deviated from the classical method slightly. In a strictly classical approach, the students are not allowed to do anything other than re-tell the original story at this level of instruction. In <u>Writing Tales</u>, the first draft of each story written by the students is a strict re-telling of the original story being studied, as in the classical method. Then, after further study of the story, the students are allowed to add creative touches of their own to the final draft. The basic story and events must stay the same; students are encouraged to add their own ideas to descriptions of characters, or further explanations as to why certain events happened, for example. When the course is completed, each student will have a "book" of 15 stories authored by them and based on well-written fables and legends.

Grammar is included, since a thorough knowledge of the English language belongs in the tool chest of every writer. During the 30 weeks of study in <u>Level One</u> the students will learn basic rules for capital letters, punctuation, quotes, both direct and indirect, and all eight parts of speech (nouns, verbs, etc.) Practice is also included in handwriting (with copywork), vocabulary and dictionary skills, and spelling.

<u>Writing Tales</u> is divided into 30 lessons, each one five days long. 15 fables, fairy tales and legends are studied and rewritten, while 15 grammar lessons are taught simultaneously. In the odd-numbered lessons the story is introduced, copywork is done, vocabulary is studied, the grammar lesson is taught and the rough draft

is done, vocabulary is studied, the grammar lesson is taught and the rough draft is written. In the even-numbered lessons spelling is practiced from mistakes in the rough draft, further study is done with the grammar lesson, additional stories are read and analyzed, and a final draft with creative touches is written. Plenty of games for review and practice are included.

A unique feature of <u>Writing Tales</u> is the inclusion of lesson plans for both homeschoolers and "co-opers." In the Homeschool Lesson Plans, each Lesson is divided into five days of instruction. The Co-op Lesson Plans include one day of instruction for each lesson, followed by four days of work to be done at home. If you are homeschooling more than one child with <u>Writing Tales,</u> you may want to consider following the Co-op Lesson Plans instead of the Homeschool Lesson Plans because of the group activities and games that are included. Also, these Lesson Plans are easily adaptable to school situations if so desired. The Teacher's Guide also includes an answer key for the student pages and two appendices. Appendix A contains additional teaching materials that will be needed, such as story sequencing strips and review games. Appendix B is a list of books recommended for additional read-alouds to be used in the even-numbered lessons.

<u>Writing Tales Level One</u> is recommended for the third or fourth grade level.

I wish you all the best as you and your students begin a journey of studying and writing the English language with <u>Writing Tales</u>.

~Amy Hastings Olsen

Many thanks must go to my family for helping me get through this project. Kids, Mom will probably not be super-glued to the computer anymore, at least for the foreseeable future! Glen, thank you for putting up with a night owl who works best after midnight. I couldn't have done this without each one of you.

I would be remiss if I did not thank three individuals, Cory Hook and Sue Rumeau of the Christian Homeschoolers Classical Co-operative in Green Pond, New Jersey, and Judith Folkerts, a homeschooling mom from Roseland, New Jersey. Their enthusiasm and praise for my work-in-progress inspired me to the finish line and warmed my heart. I must also thank my Language 3 class of 2004-2005 for being my "guinea pigs": Becky, James, Timothy, Mark C., Mark R., Daniel and Christopher. They did a great job with a rough draft of this curriculum, and they're all becoming great writers! They are also editors-in-training, and never missed a chance to point out a mistake to Mrs. Olsen. What would I have done without them!

Writing Tales – Level One
Scope & Sequence of Instruction

Lessons	Story	Grammatical Concepts
1/2	The Crow and the Pitcher	3 Requirements for a Sentence
3/4	The Town Mouse & the Country Mouse	4 kinds of sentences
5/6	Androcles	4 rules of capitalization
7/8	Julius Caesar	Punctuation Traffic Signals
9/10	The Princess & the Pea	Simple Quotes: Direct vs. Indirect
11/12	The Elves & the Shoemaker	Nouns
13/14	The Cat, the Monkey & the Chestnuts	Pronouns
15/16	How the Princess was Beaten in a Race	Verbs
17/18	Cornelia's Jewels	Adjectives
19/20	Alexander & Bucephalus	Adverbs
21/22	King Alfred and the Cakes	Prepositions
23/24	The Travels of Ching	Conjunctions
25/26	King Canute on the Seashore	Interjections
27/28	The Three Goats Named Bruse	Grammar Review
29/30	William Tell	Grammar Review

Table of Contents

Homeschool Lesson Plans

Lesson 1

Story: The Crow and the Pitcher – Aesop [e'sop]
Grammar Lesson: Three Requirements for a Sentence.

Day 1: Introduce the Crow and the Pitcher. Give background information about Aesop.

According to ancient historians, Aesop was born as a Greek slave in the area of Samos around 620 B.C. Legend has it that he was born deformed in body, but with a brilliant mind. It is said that his second master eventually freed him because of his obvious wisdom and talent. It is also reported that the citizens of Delphi were so insulted by his keen sarcasm and wit in 564 B.C. that they sentenced him to death and pushed him off a cliff. Hundreds of fables are attributed to Aesop today.

Read the Crow and the Pitcher, page 1, out loud with your child.
Discuss the story.
Who are the main characters? *(the Crow)*
What is the problem or conflict? *(he can't reach the water in the bottom of the Pitcher)*
What is the resolution? *(the Crow fills the Pitcher with pebbles one by one to raise the water up to his level)*
Have your child re-tell the story orally back to you.

Practice sequencing the events in the story by using the sentence strips found in Appendix A. Make a copy of the sentence strips. Have your student cut them apart, mix them up, and then practice putting them together in the correct story order.

Day 2: Copywork, page 2.

Introduce the Grammar Lesson by reading page 4 with your child.
Learn three ways to identify a sentence.

<<1. A sentence starts with a capital letter and ends with a punctuation mark.
        Sentences ALWAYS start with capital letters! Sentences will ALWAYS end with a period, question mark, or exclamation point.
                         .   ?   !
2. A sentence expresses a complete thought.
        Sentences are nice! They will never leave you wondering what they're talking about.

3. A sentence tells us WHO or WHAT, and WHAT THEY DID.

A sentence will always have a subject, which tells us WHO or WHAT the sentence is about. Also, a sentence will always have a verb, which tells us what the subject did.>>

Practice identifying sentences with the student. You may use the sentence strips from the ordering activity. Change some of them so they are NOT sentences, and ask the student to identify which ones are sentences, and why or why not.

Day 3: Have your child look up the vocabulary words on page 3. You may need to instruct him in basic dictionary skills, and then do this activity with him for the first few times. By Lesson 15 he should be able to do this independently. The child will use one of his vocabulary words in a sentence at the bottom of the page. Using what we have learned about sentences, discuss with the child: what makes his sentence a sentence?

Day 4: Re-read the Grammar Lesson, page 4. Use the concepts by doing Sentence Practice, pages 5-6.

Day 5: Discuss the rough draft the student will be writing today. He is to re-tell the original story in his own words. Creative touches are not allowed until the final draft is written in the next lesson. This time he must stay with the original characters and the events exactly as they happened. Rough drafts, if handwritten, must be written in pencil and not pen. Students who have difficulty with the fine motor skill of handwriting may dictate their stories to you, at your discretion. Final drafts may be dictated completely; rough drafts should be at least partially handwritten. Have him write the first two sentences by himself, for example, and then he may dictate the rest of the story; gradually increase the amount of handwriting he does each time.

The student will write his rough draft, using the instructions and checklist on page 7 to self-edit. Check over his work, making sure to note positive things as well as things that need to be changed.

Lesson 2

Story: The Crow and the Pitcher – Aesop
Grammar Lesson: Three Requirements for a Sentence.

Day 1: Review the three requirements for sentences.

Have the student open her book to "The Crow and the Pitcher." Work through the story together, looking at each sentence. Have the student circle the capital letter at the beginning of each sentence with a green crayon or pencil for "go." Have the student circle the end punctuation of each sentence with a red crayon or pencil for "stop."

Day 2: Spelling Practice, page 8.

Read together a fable of your choice from Fables by Arnold Lobel. Discuss the story with the student. Who were the main characters? What was the problem or conflict? What was the resolution? What does this fable teach us?

Day 3: Grammar Lesson – Sentences, page 9.

The student will write her final draft today, using page 10. As discussed in the workbook, now is the time that the student may add a few creative touches here or there to personalize her story. Characters may be given names, for example. Different animals or people may be used. Your job, as teacher, is to make sure the basic story stays the same. Have the student edit her final story using the checklist provided.

Check over the student's finished version, looking for spelling or grammatical errors. The final story will be re-copied on Day 5.

Day 4: More Sentence Practice, pages 11-12.

Day 5: The student will copy over the final version of her story today. Choose a special place to keep her finished stories over the year, such as a three-ring binder or a folder. At the end of the year, "publish" a book of stories written by your child!

Lesson 3

Story: "The Town Mouse and the Country Mouse" – Aesop
Grammar Lesson: Four Kinds of Sentences.

Day 1: Introduce "The Town Mouse and the Country Mouse," page 13. Read the story out loud with your child and discuss.
Who are the main characters? *(the Town Mouse and the Country Mouse)*
What is the problem or conflict? *(the Town Mouse does not like the Country Mouse's home; the Country Mouse does not like the dogs at the Town Mouse's home)*
What is the resolution? *(they decide they are each better off in their own homes and learn to be grateful for what they have)*
Have the student re-tell the story back to you orally.

Practice sequencing the events in the story by using the sentence strips from Appendix A. Make a copy of the sentences, have your student cut them apart, mix them up, and then practice putting them back together in the correct story order.

Day 2: Copywork, page 14.

Introduce the Grammar Lesson by reading page 16 with your child. Learn four kinds of sentences.

<< *There are __four__ different types of sentences.*
1. Statement – declares a fact. Statements usually end with periods.
     Now you must know that a Town Mouse once upon a time went on a visit to his cousin in the country.
2. Question – asks for information. Questions end with a question mark.
     "What is that?"
3. Command – gives an order. Commands usually end with periods, but strong commands could end with exclamation points.
     "Come you with me and I will show you how to live."
4. Exclamation – exclaims; shows emotion. Exclamations usually end with exclamation points.
     "Only!" or "What!" >>

Play a game to practice identifying different types of sentences. Get four index cards. On one write "STATEMENT." On the next write "QUESTION." On the third write "COMMAND" and on the last write "EXCLAMATION." Tape one card to each wall of the room. Read aloud the following sentences to your student. He must decide what type of sentence you have read and run to the correct wall. For example, if you read a statement, he must run to the wall with the "STATEMENT" card on it.

1. A Town Mouse once upon a time went on a visit. (S)
2. Did he visit his cousin in the country? (Q)
3. Wow! (E)
4. The Country Mouse made him heartily welcome. (S)
5. Yum! (E)
6. Did he offer his cousin food to eat? (Q)
7. Why didn't the Town Mouse like the food in the country? (Q)
8. Come with me. (C)
9. I will show you how to live. (S)
10. Set off for town at once. (C)
11. Suddenly they heard growling and barking. (S)

You may continue the game, making up your own sentences as you go.
Save the cards for later use.

Day 3: Vocabulary, page 15. After he writes a sentence using one of the words, discuss with him what kind of sentence he wrote.

Day 4: Re-read the Grammar Lesson, page 16. Use the concepts by doing Kinds of Sentences, page 17.

Day 5: Read the story again. The student will write his rough draft, using the instructions and checklist on page 18 to self-edit. Remind him of the requirements for the rough draft: a strict re-telling of the story in his own words. Save creative touches the next draft. Check over his work, making sure to note positive things as well as things that need to be changed.

* Locate a copy of <u>Fables</u> by Arnold Lobel for Lesson 4, Day 2.

Lesson 4

Story: "The Town Mouse and the Country Mouse" – Aesop
Grammar Lesson: Four Kinds of Sentences.

Day 1: Spelling Practice, page 19 and Grammar Lesson Review page 20.

Day 2: Read together a fable of your choice from <u>Fables</u> by Arnold Lobel. Discuss the story with your student. Who were the main characters? What was the problem or conflict? What was the resolution? What does this fable teach us?

Review the four types of sentences. Using the index cards from the last lesson, play the same game with sentences you choose from today's story.

Day 3: The student will write her final draft today, using page 21. As discussed in the workbook, now is the time that the student may add a few creative touches here or there to personalize her story. Characters may be given names, for example. Different animals or people may be used. Your job, as teacher, is to make sure the basic story stays the same. Have the student edit her final story using the checklist provided.

Check over the student's finished version, looking for spelling or grammatical errors. The final story will be re-copied on Day 5.

Day 4: Four Kinds of Sentences, page 22.

Day 5: The student will copy over the final version of her story today. Be sure to save it in a safe place!

Lesson 5

Story: "Androcles" [an'dr*uc*-klez] – Aesop
Grammar Lesson: Four Rules of Capitalization

Day 1: Introduce "Androcles," page 23. Read the story out loud with your child and discuss.
Who are the main characters? *(Androcles, the Lion, and the Emperor)*
What is the problem or conflict? *(Androcles is an escaped slave; the Lion has a thorn in his paw; Androcles is later sentenced to be eaten by the Lion)*
What is the resolution? *(Androcles pulls the thorn out of the Lion's paw, thus creating a lifelong friendship; later the Lion refuses to eat Androcles; after hearing the story the Emperor decides to set Androcles free)*
Have the student re-tell the story back to you orally.

Practice sequencing the events in the story by using the sentence strips from Appendix A. See Lesson 1 for suggestions.

Day 2: Copywork, page 24.

Introduce the Grammar Lesson using page 26. Learn four rules for capitalization.

<< 1. *Sentences* start with a capital letter.
  We've already learned about this rule!
2. *Titles* begin with capital letters.
  Titles like Mr., Mrs., Miss, or Dr. always start with capital letters. The important words in book, movie, story or song titles always start with capital letters. For example, our stories, "Androcles" or "The Town Mouse and the Country Mouse."
3. *Proper Names* begin with capital letters.
  Specific names of people, places or things always start with capital letters, because we want to recognize that they are special and unique. For example, the city of Boston is special and unique, so we capitalize the "B". Kristen, Timothy and Melissa are all special and unique people, so we begin their names with capital letters. And the Frisbee is a very special and unique toy, so its name starts with a capital letter too!
4. *The word* **"I"** *is always capitalized.*
  Are you special and unique? Of course you are! Then always capitalize the word "I"! >>

Play "KA-BOOM" to review four different kinds of sentences.

Set-up: Copy the "Ka-Boom" pages from Appendix A. You may wish to copy them on cardstock for durability. For additional durability, I recommend "laminating" them with clear shelf paper. Put the strips in an empty, clean potato chip can. Paste a piece of colorful paper around the barrel of the can and write "Ka-boom!" on it.

Play: Students draw strips out of the can one at a time and tell you what kind of sentence it is. If they are correct, they keep the sentence strip. If incorrect, they must put it back in the can. If they draw "Ka-boom!" they must put all of their strips back in the can. The student with the most strips at the end of the game wins. If you are playing with just one student, you may choose an amount of time to play the game and see how many strips the child has at the end of the time. Perhaps you could trade chocolate candies, peanuts or raisins – one or two for each sentence strip the child still has at the end!

Day 3: Vocabulary, page 25. After the student writes a sentence using one of the words, discuss with him what kind of sentence he wrote and where there should be capital letters.

Day 4: Re-read Grammar Lesson, page 26. Use the concepts by doing Capitalization Practice, pages 27-28.

Day 5: Read the story again. The student will write his rough draft, using the instructions and checklist on page 29 to self-edit. Remind him to stay strictly with the basic story for now. Check over his work, paying special attention to correct capitalization.

Lesson 6

Story: "Androcles" – Aesop
Grammar Lesson: Four Rules of Capitalization

Day 1: Spelling Practice, page 30 and Capitalization, page 31.

Day 2: Read together a fable of your choice from Fables by Arnold Lobel. Discuss the story with the student. Who were the main characters? What was the problem or conflict? What was the resolution? What does this fable teach us?

Use "The Town Mouse and the Country Mouse", page 13 in the student workbook, to practice capitalization rules. Your child will need four crayons or colored pencils: green, blue, red and yellow. Work through the story together, circling all the capital letters with the following instructions:

1. Circle the letter in green if the letter is at the beginning of a sentence.
2. Circle the letter in blue if it is at the beginning of a name.
3. Circle the letter in red if it is at the beginning of a title.
4. Circle the letter in yellow if it is the word "I."

Day 3: The student will write her final draft today, using page 32. As discussed before, now is the time that she may add a few creative touches here or there to personalize her story. Characters may be given names, for example. Different animals or people may be used. Check carefully to make sure the basic story stays the same and to correct any spelling or grammatical errors. Have the student edit her final story using the checklist provided. The final story will be re-copied on Day 5.

Day 4: Capitalization Review, page 33.

Play "Kaboom" to review the 4 types of sentences. Variation: Review the capitalization rules by indicating a capital letter on the sentence the student has chosen and asking for the reason why it is capitalized. If she is correct, she gets to keep the strip. If not, she must put it back and try again.

Day 5: The student will copy over the final version of her story today, with your corrections from Day 3 included. Put the final story in a safe place with her others.

Lesson 7

Story: "Julius Caesar [se'*zur*]" – James Baldwin
Grammar Lesson: Punctuation Traffic Signals

Day 1: Introduce "Julius Caesar." Give some background information on the author, James Baldwin.

James Baldwin was born in Indiana in 1841 and lived until 1925. His childhood was marked by infrequent schooling and a limited access to books. Still, his father had a "library" that consisted of two shelves of books. These books were precious to James, and developed a love of literature in him that lasted a lifetime. He grew up to become first a teacher, founding and improving many schools in Indiana. During this time he began writing. Some of the books he wrote were for teachers, but most of them were books of stories for children. He loved to re-tell old classics, and by doing this he made exciting moral tales accessible to students all over the country and helped many children develop the same love of reading that he had fostered in himself so many years before. In 1887 Baldwin moved east to join the education department of Harper & Brothers, and later the American Book Company. While editing numerous textbooks, he continued writing. At one time it was said that he had either written or edited at least half of all the textbooks being used in schools across the country!

Read "Julius Caesar," page 34-35, out loud together and discuss.
Who are the main characters? *(Julius Caesar, Caesar's officers, the boat's captain)*
What is the problem or conflict? *(the officers make fun of the village mayor; a storm threatens to capsize Caesar's boat and the captain is frightened)*
What is the resolution? *(Caesar rebukes the officer by saying it is better to be in charge of a small village than to be the second man in command of a large city; Caesar comforts the captain with his bravery in the face of the storm)*
Have the student re-tell the story back to you orally.

Practice sequencing the events in the story by using the sentence strips from Appendix A. See Lesson 1 for suggestions.

Day 2: Copywork, page 36.

Introduce the Grammar Lesson using page 38.
The student will learn Punctuation Traffic Signals.

<< For this grammar lesson, let's think of punctuation as the traffic signals in our writing. The punctuation marks tell us when to slow down and when to stop, and help to keep our words from bumping into each other.
<u>*The Red Lights:*</u> *These are the easy ones, and we've already learned them! Think of the period, the exclamation point, and the question mark as "red lights." When you see them, the sentence stops! Don't start moving again until you see the "green light" of the next sentence's beginning capital letter.*
<u>*The Yield Signs:*</u> *Commas act like yield signs; they tell you to slow down before proceeding. Take a breath, look around, and then continue on with your journey of reading the sentence.*
<u>*The Stop Signs:*</u> *Semi-colons act like stop signs. They tell the reader to slow down and stop before continuing on again.>>*

Put the new grammatical concepts into practice by playing "Red Light, Green Light." This game works best with three or more players, but may be adapted to be played with only two (teacher and student) as well. One player is the Traffic Cop and stands at one end of the room. The other players line up at the other end. The Traffic Cop calls out "Capital Letter!" (instead of "Green Light") when he wants the other players to start moving. The other players walk towards the Traffic Cop. The Traffic Cop can call out "Exclamation Point!" or "Period!" or

"Question Mark!" when he wants the other players to stop. He may then start them up again by calling "Capital Letter!" The Traffic Cop may also call out, "Comma!" at which point the students must stop, say "Take a break!" and then continue on. If the Traffic Cop catches anyone not following his instructions, he may send them back to start. The first student to reach the Traffic Cop becomes the next Traffic Cop.

Day 3: Vocabulary, page 37. After he writes a sentence using one of the words, discuss with him what kind of sentence he wrote and which "traffic signals", or punctuation, he used.

Day 4: Re-read Grammar Lesson, page 38. Use the concepts by doing Punctuation Practice, page 39.

Day 5: Read the story again. The student will write his rough draft, using the instructions and checklist on page 40 to self-edit. Remind him to stay strictly with the events of the original story. Check over his work, paying special attention to correct capitalization and punctuation.

* Locate a copy of Punctuation Takes a Vacation for Lesson 8, Day 2

Lesson 8

Story: "Julius Caesar" – James Baldwin
Grammar Lesson: Punctuation Traffic Signals

Day 1: Spelling Practice, page 41 and Punctuation Review, page 42.

Day 2: Read together Punctuation Takes a Vacation by Robin Pulver. Discuss the story with your student. What happened when the punctuation marks left for vacation? Did the words that were left behind know how to behave?

Play "Red Light, Green Light" again to review the concepts of punctuation.

Day 3: The student will begin her final draft today, using page 43. This is the time that she may add some creative touches. Please note: as discussed in the workbook on page 43, special care must be taken with this story, since it is about a real person and actual events. Limit creativity to small things such as describing the village people who witnessed Caesar going by or adding detail to the Roman soldier who commented to Caesar about the people. Have the student edit her final story using the checklist provided. Check her story over carefully, making sure the basic story stays the same and correcting any spelling, grammatical or mechanical errors. The final story will be re-copied on Day 5.

Day 4: Will the Real Punctuation Please Stand Up?, page 44-45.

Play "Kaboom" to review the 4 types of sentences. Variation: Review the punctuation rules by indicating a punctuation mark on the sentence that the student has chosen and asking for the "movement" that the "traffic signal" tells; i.e., stop, pause, stop and then move on.

Day 5: The student will copy over the final version of her story today, with your corrections from Day 3 included. Put the final story in a safe place with her others, and remember to share her finished work with the rest of your family from time to time.

Lesson 9

Story: "The Princess and the Pea" – Hans Christian Andersen
Grammar Lesson: Simple Quotes: Direct vs. Indirect and Punctuation

Day 1: Introduce "The Princess and the Pea." Give some background information on the author, Hans Christian Andersen.

Hans Christian Andersen was born in 1805 in the slums of Odense, Denmark. His mother was a washerwoman and his father a poor shoemaker. Andersen had very little education until he was older, but when he was a young boy his father, who loved literature, did much to encourage Andersen's love of stories and fairy tales. He took him to see plays, encouraged him to make up stories, and read to him, often from "Arabian Nights." After a failed attempt at a dramatic career, Andersen was granted tuition to a local grammar school (where he studied with 11 year olds even though he was 17!) and then later to Copenhagen University. He became a successful writer and poet. His most famous book has always been "Fairy Tales and Stories." In a time when other writers made their fortune by re-writing old folk tales, only 12 of Andersen's 156 fairy tales were not original.

Read "The Princess and the Pea," pages 46-47, out loud with the students and discuss.
Who are the main characters? *(the prince, the princess, the old queen)*
What is the problem or conflict? *(the prince needs to marry a princess but he has difficulty finding a real one)*

What is the resolution? *(the queen puts a pea underneath the princess' mattresses as a test to see if she is a genuine princess)*
Have the students re-tell the story back to you orally.

Practice sequencing the events in the story by using the sentence strips from Appendix A. See Lesson 1 for suggestions.

Day 2: Copywork, page 48.

Introduce the Grammar Lesson using pages 50-51.
The students will learn about Simple Quotes.

<< *When we talk about quotes in a story, we are talking about words that people are saying.*
Direct Quotes *are words that the character is actually saying, and are always surrounded by quotation marks.*

> *Example: "Ouch!" cried the princess.*

Indirect Quotes *are words that the storyteller tells us were said by the characters. They do not have quotation marks.*

> *Example: The princess cried out in pain. or The princess said that she did not*
> *sleep well the night before.*

-Indirect quotes are easy to punctuate; use the same rules we learned for regular sentences. Begin with a capital letter, use commas if you want the reader to pause, semi-colons if you want the reader to stop and then continue on, and always end with a period, exclamation point or question mark.
-Direct quotes can be more difficult to punctuate.
-The words actually said by a character must be surrounded by quotation marks.

> *"I don't think this bed is very comfortable."*

-The words inside the quotation marks will start with a beginning capital letter, just like a sentence.
-If the narrator introduces the quote (She said, "Ouch!"), there will be a comma before the quotation marks, because you want the reader to pause before reading the quote, and end punctuation at the end <u>inside the quotation marks</u> *to show that the sentence is finished.*

> *He asked, "Why didn't you sleep well?"*

-If the narrator finishes the quote instead ("Ouch," she said.) AND the quote from the character was a sentence that should end in a period, then a comma is put at the end of the quote, inside the quotation marks, so that there will be a pause before finishing the sentence, and the end punctuation will be put at the end, after the narrator concludes the sentence.

> *"I need more mattresses," said the queen.*

-If the character says in a direct quote something that would end with an exclamation point or a question mark, these are left in the quote, and the sentence will still end with an end punctuation mark after the narrator finishes it.

"Why didn't you sleep well?" he asked.
"Goodness gracious!" she cried. >>

Please note – this is a rather difficult grammar lesson! Concentrate on teaching your student to distinguish between direct and indirect quotes. Punctuation within quotes may be corrected as needed in the student's stories throughout the year and will be mastered gradually.

Put the new grammatical concepts into practice by playing a new version of "Kaboom", using the "Simple Quotes" sentence strips in Appendix A. Copy these strips on a different color paper from the first set of sentences so you have two sets to play with – the first set for identifying kinds of sentences, the second set for identifying kinds of quotes. Play with the second set of sentences today. The student will draw a sentence strip and tell you whether the sentence contains a direct quote or an indirect quote. As before, if he is right, he keeps the strip. If he draws "Kaboom!", he must put all of his strips back in the can.

Day 3: Vocabulary, page 49. After the student writes a sentence using one of the words, discuss with him what kind of sentence he wrote and which "traffic signals", or punctuation, he used.

Day 4: Re-read Grammar Lesson, pages 50-51. Use the concepts by doing Quotations, page 52.

Day 5: Read the story again. The student will write his rough draft, using the instructions and checklist on page 53 to self-edit. Remind him to stay strictly with the events of the original story for this first writing. Check over his work, paying special attention to correct capitalization and punctuation.

* Locate a copy of <u>Squids Will be Squids</u> by Jon Scieszka for Lesson 10, Day 2.

Lesson 10

Story: "The Princess and the Pea," Hans Christian Andersen
Grammar Lesson: Simple Quotes: Direct vs. Indirect and Punctuation

Day 1: Spelling Practice, page 54 and Practice with Simple Quotes, page 55.

Day 2: Choose a fable from Squids Will Be Squids by John Scieszka to read together. Discuss: what is the moral? What can we learn from this story? These stories are wonderful, but short, so you may decide to read two or three.

Play "Kaboom" again with the second set of sentences to review Direct vs. Indirect Quotes. Variation: if your students seem to be grasping the concept easily, have them not only identify the kind of quote, but also change the sentence from a direct to an indirect quote or vice versa.

Day 3: The student will begin her final draft today, using page 56. Now she may add some creativity to her story. Ideas for creative touches are in the student workbook. Have the student edit her final story using the checklist provided. Check her story carefully; making sure the basic story stays the same and correcting any spelling, grammatical or other mechanical errors. The final story will be re-copied on Day 5.

Day 4: Quotations, pages 57-58 and Grammar Review, page 59.

Play "Red Light, Green Light" to review Punctuation Traffic Signals.

Day 5: The student will copy over the final version of her story today, with your corrections from Day 3 included. Put the final story in a safe place with her others, but consider sharing it with family and friends first.

Lesson 11

Story: "The Elves and the Shoemaker" – Horace E. Scudder
Grammar Lesson: Nouns

Day 1: Introduce "The Elves and the Shoemaker." Give some background information on the author, Horace E. Scudder.

Horace E. Scudder (1838-1902) was a very popular children's author of the nineteenth century. His most popular books were The Book of Fables, The Book of Folk Stories, The

Book of Legends and _Fables and Folk Stories_. He worked hard to have good literature introduced into schools. For this reason, he wrote numerous historical and biographical works, including a biography of George Washington that is still considered to be the finest ever written for children.

Read "The Elves and the Shoemaker," pages 60-61, out loud with your student and discuss.
Who are the main characters? _(the Shoemaker and his wife, the Elves)_
What is the problem or conflict? _(the Shoemaker is running out of money)_
What is the resolution? _(the Elves make beautiful shoes for the Shoemaker to sell; the Shoemaker's wife makes clothes for the Elves to say thank you)_
Have the students re-tell the story back to you orally.

Make a copy of the "Storyboard" page from Appendix A. Read the story one more time and have your child draw simple pictures of the events as they happen.

Day 2: Copywork, page 62.

Introduce the Grammar Lesson using page 64.
The students will learn about Nouns.

_<< A _noun_ is the name of a person, place, thing, or idea._
Examples: People – elves, shoemaker, customer, wife
Places – shop, village, workroom, street
Things – shoe, leather, stitch, curtain, bench
Ideas – honesty, love, hope, wonder, troubles
Most nouns are called Common Nouns. Nouns that name specific people or places are called Proper Nouns. Proper Nouns always start with capital letters.
Example: Sally, John, Mr. Jones, Seattle, Boston >>

This is a fairly easy grammar lesson. The hardest part of learning nouns is to grasp the concept of nouns as names of ideas. Pay special attention to this, but don't get stuck on it if your student has trouble. This idea will sink in as he gets older and can better comprehend abstract concepts such as _hope, love, honesty,_ or _fate._

Put the new grammatical concepts into practice by playing "Name That Noun" together. Copy and hand out the game page from Appendix A. Play with one column at a time. The first round will be "Persons". You will each have two minutes to write down as many nouns for "persons" that you can think of. You may either play to see how many each of you can come up with, or you may compare your lists, cross out the duplicates, and only score points for the original nouns. Play again with "Places," "Things," and "Ideas."

Day 3: Vocabulary, page 63. After the student writes a sentence using one of the words, discuss with him what kind of sentence he wrote and identify the nouns in it.

Day 4: Re-read Grammar Lesson, page 64. Use the concepts by doing Nouns, page 65.

Day 5: Read the story again. The student will write his rough draft, using the instructions and checklist on page 66 to self-edit. Remind him to stay strictly with the events of the original story this time. Check over his work, paying special attention to correct capitalization and punctuation.

Lesson 12

Story: "The Elves and the Shoemaker," by Horace E. Scudder
Grammar Lesson: Nouns

Day 1: Spelling Practice, page 67 and Noun Practice, page 68.

Day 2: Choose a fable from Fables by Arnold Lobel to read together. Discuss: Who are the main characters? What is the main problem/conflict? How is it solved? What is the moral? What can we learn from this story?

Go through "The Elves and the Shoemaker" together in the workbooks, circling all the nouns in purple. You may also choose to review concepts by circling beginning capital letters in green, end punctuation in red, and quotation marks, commas and semi-colons in blue.

Day 3: The student will begin her final draft today, using page 69. Now is the time she may add some creativity to her story. Ideas for creative touches are in the student workbook. Have the student edit her final story using the checklist provided. Check her story carefully; making sure the basic story stays the same and correcting any spelling, grammatical or other mechanical errors. The final story will be re-copied on Day 5.

Day 4: The Eight Parts of Speech, page 70, and Grammar Review, pages 71-72.

Play another round of "Name That Noun," OR "Kaboom!" OR "Red Light, Green Light."

Day 5: The student will copy over the final version of her story today, with your corrections from Day 3 included. Put the final story in a safe place with the others.

Lesson 13

Story: "The Cat, the Monkey and the Chestnuts" – Horace E. Scudder
Grammar Lesson: Pronouns

Day 1: Introduce "The Cat, the Monkey and the Chestnuts."
Read "The Cat, the Monkey and the Chestnuts," page 73, out loud together and discuss.
Who are the main characters? *(the Cat and the Monkey)*
What is the problem or conflict? *(they want to get the chestnuts out of the hot ashes to eat them)*
What is the resolution? *(the Monkey flatters the Cat into getting the chestnuts out of the hot ashes, the Monkey eats them while the Cat is getting them out)*
Have the student re-tell the story back to you orally.

Use the "Storyboard" page from Appendix A to practice sequencing the story. Read the story one more time, having the child draw simple pictures of the events as they happen.

Day 2: Copywork, page 74.

Introduce the Grammar Lesson using page 76.
The student will learn about Pronouns.

*<< A **pronoun** is a word that takes the place of a noun.*
Examples: I, you, he, she, it, we, they, my, mine, me, our, them
In the title of our story, there are three nouns:
        *"The **Cat**, the **Monkey**, and the **Chestnuts**"*
If we replaced each noun with a pronoun, our silly title would look like this:
        *"**She**, **He**, and **Them**"*
It's a good thing we have nouns, so we know what we are talking about! Pronouns are important too; they keep our writing from sounding awkward.
Look at this sentence from our story, with all nouns and no pronouns:

Scarcely had the Cat touched the hot ashes than the Cat drew back with a cry, for the Cat had burned the Cat's paw.

Now here it is again, with pronouns put back in:

Scarcely had the Cat touched the hot ashes than <u>she</u> drew back with a cry, for <u>she</u> had burned <u>her</u> paw.

It sounds much better! >>

Review the definition of a noun and practice the definition of a pronoun. You may choose to have your student write the definitions on index cards for further practice.

Put the new grammatical concepts into practice by playing "ID Tic Tac Toe" together. Copy the word page (Nouns and Pronouns) from Appendix A onto stiff card stock, cut into word squares and put into a bag. On his turn, the player will pull a word square from the bag and must identify it as either a noun or a pronoun. If he is correct, he may place an X or an O onto a tic tac toe board. If he is incorrect, he forfeits his turn.

Day 3: Vocabulary, page 75. After he writes a sentence using one of the words, discuss with him what kind of sentence he wrote and identify any nouns or pronouns in it.

Day 4: Re-read Grammar Lesson, page 76. Use the concepts by doing Pronouns, page 77.

Day 5: Read the story again. The student will write his rough draft, using the instructions and checklist on page 78 to self-edit. Check over his work, making sure that he has stayed strictly with the events of the original story and has correct capitalization and punctuation.

Lesson 14

Story: "The Cat, the Monkey and the Chestnuts," by Horace E. Scudder
Grammar Lesson: Pronouns

Day 1: Spelling Practice, page 79 and Pronoun Practice, page 80. You may choose to play "Tic Tac Toe" again to review identifying nouns and pronouns.

Day 2: Choose a fable from <u>Squids Will Be Squids</u> to read together. Discuss: Who are the main characters? What is the main problem/conflict? How is it solved? What is the moral? What can we learn from this story?

Review the definitions of nouns and pronouns. Work on getting your student to memorize them. You may put the definition to a silly rhythm and then march around the room with her chanting it. You may choose to write the definition on a blackboard or white board, then say it together repeatedly, having your student erase one word each time until you are both saying the definition without any words written on the board.

Go through the story together in the workbooks, circling all the nouns in purple and the pronouns in yellow. You may also choose to review past concepts by circling beginning capital letters in green, end punctuation in red, and quotation marks, commas and semi-colons in blue.

Day 3: The student will begin her final draft today, using page 81. Now she may add some creativity to her story. Ideas for creative touches are in the student workbook. Have the student edit her final story using the checklist provided. Check her story carefully; making sure the basic story stays the same and correcting any mechanical errors. The final story will be re-copied on Day 5.

Day 4: Parts of Speech chart, page 82 and More Pronouns, page 83.

Play "Name That Noun," OR "Kaboom!" OR "Red Light, Green Light."

Day 5: The student will copy over the final version of her story today, with your corrections from Day 3 included. Put the final story in a safe place with the others.

Lesson 15

Story: "How the Princess was Beaten in a Race" – Horace E. Scudder
Grammar Lesson: Verbs

Day 1: Introduce "How the Princess was Beaten in a Race."
Read "How the Princess was Beaten in a Race," pages 84-85, out loud together and discuss.
Who are the main characters? *(the princess and the poor young man)*
What is the problem or conflict? *(the young man must beat the princess in a race in order to marry her)*
What is the resolution? *(the young man uses various tricks to distract the princess so that he can beat her in the race)*
Have the student re-tell the story back to you orally.
Practice sequencing the events in the story by using the sentence strips from Appendix A. See Lesson 1 for suggestions.

Day 2: Copywork, page 86.

Review the definitions of nouns and pronouns.

Introduce the Grammar Lesson using page 88.
The student will learn about verbs.

<<A verb is a word that shows an action or a state of being.
There are two kinds of verbs we will learn about:
Action Verbs – An action verb is a word that shows an action, like run, walk, eat, think, chew, and study.
Here's an easy test for action verbs: If you can put the word in the sentence, "I can _____," and it makes sense, then it is an action verb.
For example, "I can run." "I can walk." "I can think." "I can study."
State of Being Verbs – A state-of-being verb is a word that states that something IS. For example, "Melissa IS smart." "Timothy IS funny." "Kristen IS beautiful." "He WAS tired." "They WERE in the pool." "I AM happy."
You can remember the eight state-of-being verbs with a little chant. The rhythm goes like this: slow, slow, quick-quick, slow, slow, slow, slow.
Now add the following words: is, am, were-was, are, be, being, been. >>

You may wish to have your student write the definition of a verb on an index card to add to his other cards for practice.

Note: For the purposes of this level, we will stick with two simple kinds of verbs: action and state-of-being. Helping verbs will be taught at more advanced levels.

Practice the concept of action verbs by playing Verb Charades: Together brainstorm for three minutes and make a list of as many action verbs as you can. Then illustrate that these verbs show action by playing charades. Have the student secretly choose an action verb from the list and then act it out while you guess which one it is. Then switch.

Practice the State-of-Being Verbs chant together. An audio file of this chant can be found at :
http://www.kyrene.k12.az.us/schools/brisas/sunda/verb/verbs.wav

The chant is sung like this, in a singsong voice:

"is,	am,	were - was - are,	be,	being,	been."
slow,	*slow,*	*quick – quick - slow, slow,*	*slow,*	*slow.*	
clap,	*clap,*	*clap - clap - clap, clap,*	*clap,*	*clap.*	

Day 3: Vocabulary, page 87. After he writes a sentence using one of the words, discuss with him what kind of sentence he wrote and identify any nouns, pronouns or verbs in it.

Day 4: Re-read Grammar Lesson, page 88. Use the concepts by doing Verbs, page 89.

Day 5: Read the story again. The student will write his rough draft, using the instructions and checklist on page 90 to self-edit. Check over his work, making sure that he has stayed strictly with the events of the original story and has correct capitalization and punctuation.

Lesson 16

Story: "How the Princess was Beaten in a Race" – Horace E. Scudder
Grammar Lesson: Verbs

Day 1: Spelling Practice, page 91 and Verb Practice, page 92. Review the definitions of nouns, pronouns and verbs. You may choose to play Verb Charades again to review identifying action verbs.

Day 2: Review the concepts of action and state-of-being verbs by reading the stories of Action Anna and Stanley State-of-Being, found in Appendix A.

Play "Kaboom," or "Name That Noun" to review past grammatical concepts, if time.

Day 3: The student will begin her final draft today, using page 93. Now she may add some creativity to her story. Ideas for creative touches are in the student workbook. Have the student edit her final story using the checklist provided. Check her story carefully; making sure the basic events stay the same and correcting any mechanical errors. The final story will be re-copied on Day 5.

Day 4: Parts of Speech chart, page 94 and Grammar Review, page 95.

You may choose to play Grammar Tic-Tac-Toe to practice the definitions: A player must give you the definition you ask for correctly before placing an X or O on the board. If she is wrong, play forfeits to the other player. Ask the three definitions, noun, pronoun and verb, mixing them up, for one round of the game.

Day 5: The student will copy over the final versions of her story today, with your corrections from Day 3 included. Put the final story in a safe place with her others.

Lesson 17

Story: "Cornelia's Jewels" – James Baldwin
Grammar Lesson: Adjectives

Day 1: Introduce "Cornelia's Jewels."
Read "Cornelia's Jewels," pages 96-97, out loud with the students and discuss.
Who are the main characters? *(the two sons, the mother and her friend)*
What is the problem or conflict? *(the boys wish their mother could have fine jewels)*
What is the resolution? *(the mother calls her sons her jewels)*
Have the students re-tell the story back to you orally.

Practice sequencing the events in the story by using the sentence strips from Appendix A. See Lesson 1 for suggestions.

Day 2: Copywork, page 98.

Review the definitions of nouns, pronouns and verbs. Practice the State-of-Being Verbs chant together.

Introduce the Grammar Lesson using page 100.
The student will learn about adjectives.

<< An **_adjective_** *is a word that "decorates" a noun or a pronoun.*
Adjectives add color to our writing!
Consider the first two sentences of "Cornelia's Jewels". First, let's read them without any adjectives:
> *It was morning in the city of Rome years ago. In a house in a garden, two boys were standing.*
Now let's read them with the adjectives:
> *It was a bright morning in the old city of Rome many hundred years ago. In a vine-covered summer-house in a beautiful garden, two boys were standing.*
Stories are much more interesting when they have adjectives added in. The reader can picture the scene just as the author intended, and will find the story much more enjoyable.>>

You may wish to have your student write the definition of an adjective on an index card to add to his other cards for practice.

Practice the concept of adjectives by playing the Necklace Game: Use the five pictures of necklaces from Appendix A. Ask your student to secretly choose one of the necklace pictures, and then describe it to you using only adjectives. Your job is to guess which necklace he is describing. Repeat as time allows.

Day 3: Vocabulary, page 99.

Day 4: Re-read Grammar Lesson, page 100. Use the concepts by doing Adjectives, page 101.

Day 5: Read the story again. The student will write his rough draft, using the instructions and checklist on page 102 to self-edit. Check over his work, making sure that he has stayed strictly with the events of the original story and has correct capitalization and punctuation.

* Locate a copy of Where the Sidewalk Ends by Shel Silverstein for Lesson 18, Day 1.

Lesson 18

Story: "Cornelia's Jewels" – James Baldwin
Grammar Lesson: Adjectives

Day 1: Spelling Practice, page 103 and Adjective Practice, page 104. Review the definitions of nouns, pronouns, verbs and adjectives.

Choose two or three poems from Where the Sidewalk Ends by Shel Silverstein to read together.

Day 2: Review the definitions of nouns, pronouns, verbs and adjectives. Review the State-of-Being Verbs Chant.

Play ID Tic Tac Toe with the word cards to practice identifying parts of speech. Add word cards of verbs and adjectives from Appendix A, so the student will be identifying nouns, pronouns, verbs and adjectives in the game.

Day 3: The student will begin her final draft today, using page 105. Now she may add her own creative touches to the story. Ideas are in the student workbook. Have the student edit her final story using the checklist provided. Check her story carefully, making sure the basic story stays the same and correcting any mechanical errors. The final story will be re-copied on Day 5.

Day 4: Parts of Speech Chart, page 106 and Grammar Review, page 107.

Play "Kaboom,", "Verb Charades," or "Name That Noun" to review past grammatical concepts.

Day 5: The student will copy over the final version of her story today, with your corrections from Day 3 included. Put the final story in a safe place with her others.

Lesson 19

Story: "Alexander and Bucephalus [byOOse′fu*lus*]" – James Baldwin
Grammar Lesson: Adverbs

Day 1: Introduce "Alexander and Bucephalus."
Read "Alexander and Bucephalus," pages 108-109, out loud with the students and discuss.
Who are the main characters? *(King Philip, Bucephalus, Alexander)*
What is the problem or conflict? *(Bucephalus is a wild horse and will not let any of the king's men ride him)*
What is the resolution? *(Alexander notices that the horse is afraid of his own shadow; he rides him; they become inseparable and Alexander goes on to become Alexander the Great)*
Have the student re-tell the story back to you orally.

Rewrite a simple version of the story together using strictly nouns/pronouns and verbs. Then together decide where to "decorate" your story by adding adjectives.

Day 2: Copywork, page 110.
Review the definitions of nouns, pronouns, verbs and adjectives. Practice the State-of-Being Verbs chant together.

Introduce the Grammar Lesson using page 112.
The student will learn about adverbs.

<< An **_adverb_** is a word that "decorates" a verb.

Adverbs also add color to our writing, just like adjectives!

Most _adverbs end in –ly. For example: He ran quickly. She gave money generously. Sally jumped easily over the creek. Few don't, such as outside, tomorrow, there, then or more._

Adverbs answer the questions, "When?" "Where?", "How?" and "How much?"

For example, When did he run? He ran recently.

Where did he run? He ran outside.

How did he run? He ran quickly.

How much did he run? He ran occasionally. >>

You may wish to have your student write the definition of an adverb on an index card to add to his other cards for practice.

Day 3: Vocabulary, page 111.

Play Grammar Tic-Tac-Toe to practice the definitions: Each player must give you the part of speech definition you ask for correctly before placing an X or O on the board. If they are wrong, play forfeits to the other player. Ask for definitions of nouns, pronouns, verbs, adjectives and adverbs, mixing them up, for one round of the game.

Day 4: Re-read Grammar Lesson, page 112. Adverbs, page 113.

Day 5: Read the story again. The student will write his rough draft, using the instructions and checklist on page 114 to self-edit. Check over his work, making sure that he has stayed strictly with the events of the original story and has correct capitalization, spelling and punctuation.

Lesson 20

Story: "Alexander and Bucephalus" – James Baldwin
Grammar Lesson: Adverbs

Day 1: Spelling Practice, page 115 and Adverb Practice, page 116. Review the definitions of nouns, pronouns, verbs, adjectives and adverbs.

Day 2: Choose a fable from Squids Will Be Squids to read together. Discuss: Who are the main characters? What is the main problem/conflict? How is it solved? What is the moral? What can we learn from this story?

Together, re-write a simple version of the fable, using only nouns/pronouns and verbs. Next add adjectives and adverbs to "decorate" the story. Use a different color marker or pen to add the "decorating words."

Review the definitions of nouns, pronouns, verbs, adjectives and adverbs. Review the State-of-Being Verbs Chant.

Day 3: The student will begin her final draft today, using page 117. Now she may add her own creative touches to the story. Ideas are in the student workbook. Have the student edit her final story using the checklist provided. Check her story carefully; making sure the basic story stays the same and correcting any mechanical errors. The final story will be re-copied on Day 5.

Day 4: Parts of Speech Chart, page 118 and Grammar Review, pages 119-120.

Play "Kaboom,", "Verb Charades," or "Name That Noun" to review past grammatical concepts.

Day 5: The student will copy over the final version of her story today, with your corrections from Day 3 included. Put the final story in a safe place with her others.

Lesson 21

Story: "King Alfred and the Cakes" – James Baldwin
Grammar Lesson: Prepositions

Day 1: Introduce "King Alfred and the Cakes."
Read "King Alfred and the Cakes," pages 121-122, out loud together and discuss.
Who are the main characters? (*King Alfred, the woodcutter's wife*)
What is the problem or conflict? (*the King is so distracted by fighting the Danes that he forgets to watch the cakes; they burn*)
What is the resolution? (*the woodcutter's wife scolds the King; the King is amused at being scolded by her; he goes on to beat the Danes in a great battle*)
Have the student re-tell the story back to you orally.

Day 2: Copywork, page 123.

Review the definitions of nouns, pronouns, verbs, adjectives and adverbs. Practice the State-of-Being Verbs chant together.

Introduce the Grammar Lesson using page 125.

The student will learn about prepositions.

<< A **_preposition_** is a word that relates a noun or pronoun to other words in a sentence. An easy way to identify a preposition is to ask if the word is something a squirrel can do to a tree! For example, the squirrel can go near the tree, around the tree, over the tree, beside the tree, through the tree (imagine the tree is hollow) and under the tree.
Memorize this song to the tune of "Yankee Doodle". It will help you remember 28 different prepositions.

Yankee Doodle Prepositions
Above, across, after, around,
And then comes at;
Before, behind, below, beside,
Between and by.
Down and during, for and from,
In, inside and into;
Of, off, on, out, over, through,
To, under, up and with! >>

Demonstrate the concept of "what a squirrel can do to a tree" with a stuffed animal. Brainstorm! Ask your student, "What can a squirrel do to a tree?" and write his answers down, thus creating a list of prepositions together.

You may wish to have your student write the definition of a preposition on an index card to add to his other cards for practice.

Day 3: Vocabulary, page 124.

Practice "Yankee Doodle Prepositions."

Play ID Tic-Tac-Toe to practice identifying different parts of speech. Add the adverb and preposition cards from Appendix A to the game.

Day 4: Re-read Grammar Lesson, page 125. Complete Prepositions, page 126. Practice "Yankee Doodle Prepositions."

Day 5: Read the story again. The student will write his rough draft, using the instructions and checklist on page 127 to self-edit. Check over his work, making sure that he has stayed strictly with the events of the original story and has correct capitalization, spelling and punctuation.

Lesson 22

Story: "King Alfred and the Cakes" – James Baldwin
Grammar Lesson: Prepositions

Day 1: Spelling Practice, page 128 and Preposition Practice, page 129. Review the definitions of nouns, pronouns, verbs, adjectives, adverbs and prepositions. Practice "Yankee Doodle Prepositions."

Day 2: Choose two or three poems from Where the Sidewalk Ends by Shel Silverstein to read together.

Review the State-of-Being Verbs Chant and "Yankee Doodle Prepositions."

Do "King Alfred and the Cakes Fun with Parts of Speech" Activity from Appendix A.

Day 3: The student will begin her final draft today, using page 130. Now she may add her own creative touches to the story. Ideas are in the student workbook. Have the student edit her final story using the checklist provided. Check her story carefully; making sure the basic story stays the same and correcting any mechanical errors. The final story will be re-copied on Day 5.

Day 4: Parts of Speech chart, page 131 and Grammar Review, pages 132-133.

Play "Grammar Tic Tac Toe", "ID Tic Tac Toe", "Kaboom," or "Name That Noun" to review past grammatical concepts, if time.

Day 5: The student will copy over the final version of her story today, with your corrections from Day 3 included. Put the final story in a safe place with her others.

Lesson 23

Story: "The Travels of Ching" – Robert Bright
Grammar Lesson: Conjunctions

Day 1: Introduce "The Travels of Ching."

Robert Bright (1902-1988) was a popular children's author of the twentieth century. He wrote the popular "Georgie" books among others.

Read "The Travels of Ching," page 134-136, out loud together and discuss.
Who are the main characters? *(Ching and the little girl)*
What is the problem or conflict? *(the little girl cannot afford to buy Ching; Ching can not find a home)*
What is the resolution? *(the little girl's uncle in America buys Ching and sends him to his niece in China...the same little girl; the little girl and Ching are happy together)*

Look at a globe or a map to see just how far Ching traveled before he found his home.

Have the student re-tell the story back to you orally.

Use the sentence strips from Appendix A to practice sequencing the events of the story; save the strips for the conjunction activity on Day 2.

Day 2: Copywork, page 137.

Review the definitions of nouns, pronouns, verbs, adjectives, adverbs and prepositions. Practice the State-of-Being Verbs chant and "Yankee Doodle Prepositions" together.

Introduce the Grammar Lesson using page 139.
The student will learn about conjunctions.

*<< A **conjunction** is a joining word that connects words or phrases together.*
The most popular conjunction is the word "and."
"And" is as powerful as super-glue!
It can connect words, like "bat and ball," "milk and cookies," or "King Alfred and the Cakes."
It can also connect phrases. "She took Ching out on the terrace and left him sitting on the edge." "One day a Chinese laundry man came by and bought Ching."
The word "and" can even connect sentences: "Outside a wise old Chinese owl looked in

and the moon shone."

Other popular conjunctions are "but" and "or." "The rubbish man took Ching to his rubbish yard but he had to put him in a separate place." "Ching did not find a home at the tea merchants or hanging in the tree or in the rubbish can."

Other words that can be used as conjunctions are "after" "until" "therefore" or "however." >>

To demonstrate the "joining" function of conjunctions, rip a piece of paper in half, then tape it together. The tape is the "conjunction" and the paper represents words or phrases.

Next have your student choose two sentences from the sequencing activity. Write the words "and" or "but" on pieces of masking tape. He will connect the two sentences with one of the tape pieces, so a new, longer sentence is made out of the two shorter sentences that will now be joined with a conjunction.

You may wish to have the student write the definition of a conjunction on an index card to add to his other cards for practice at home.

Day 3: Vocabulary, page 138.

Play "Grammar Tic Tac Toe", "ID Tic Tac Toe", "Kaboom," or "Name That Noun" to review past grammatical concepts.

Day 4: Re-read Grammar Lesson, page 139. Complete Conjunctions, page 140.

Day 5: Read the story again. The student will write his rough draft, using the instructions and checklist on page 141 to self-edit. Check over his work, making sure that he has stayed strictly with the events of the original story and has correct capitalization, spelling and punctuation.

Lesson 24

Story: "The Travels of Ching" – Robert Bright
Grammar Lesson: Conjunctions

Day 1: Spelling Practice, page 142 and Conjunction Practice, page 143.

Review the definitions of nouns, pronouns, verbs, adjectives, adverbs, prepositions and conjunctions. Practice "Yankee Doodle Prepositions."

Day 2: Choose a fable from <u>Fables</u> by Arnold Lobel to read together. Discuss: Who are the main characters? What is the main problem/conflict? How is it solved? What is the moral? What can we learn from this story?

Review the definitions of nouns, pronouns, verbs, adjectives, adverbs, prepositions and conjunctions. Review the State-of-Being Verbs Chant and "Yankee Doodle Prepositions."

Do the Silly Sentence activity from Appendix A orally together. Students will have fun making silly sentences by combining the different phrases and conjunctions.

Day 3: The student will begin her final draft today, using pages 144-145. Now she may add her own creative touches to the story. Ideas are in the student workbook. Have the student edit her final story using the checklist provided. Check her story carefully; making sure the basic story stays the same and correcting any mechanical errors. The final story will be re-copied on Day 5.

Day 4: Parts of Speech chart, page 146 and Grammar Review, page 147.

Play "Grammar Tic Tac Toe", "ID Tic Tac Toe", "Kaboom," or "Name That Noun" to review past grammatical concepts, if time.

Day 5: The student will copy over the final version of her story today, with your corrections from Day 3 included. Put the final story in a safe place with her others.

Lesson 25

Story: "King Canute on the Seashore" – James Baldwin
Grammar Lesson: Interjections

Day 1: Introduce "King Canute on the Seashore."
Read "King Canute on the Seashore," pages 148-149, out loud together and discuss.
Who are the main characters? *(King Canute, the King's officers)*
What is the problem or conflict? *(the officers praise King Canute and his power too much)*
What is the resolution? *(King Canute tries to command the sea to stop coming in; he fails and demonstrates to the officers that no one is as powerful as God)*
Have the student re-tell the story back to you orally.

Review the definitions of nouns, pronouns, verbs, adjectives, adverbs, prepositions and conjunctions. Practice the State-of-Being Verbs chant and "Yankee Doodle Prepositions" together.

Day 2: Copywork, page 150.

Introduce the Grammar Lesson using page 152.
The student will learn about interjections.

<< *An **interjection** is a word or phrase that expresses surprise or emotion. Interjections are usually followed by either commas or exclamation points.*
> ***Hey**, what's the king doing?*
> ***Wow!** The king's going to get wet!*
> ***Oh no!** The tide is coming in!*
> ***O king**, you are the greatest.*
> *Here are some examples of other common interjections: Hooray! Alas. Unreal! Oh! Ah! Hmmm. Whoops!*>>

Brainstorm as many interjections as you can together and write them down.

Play "Jumping Interjections." Toss a ball back and forth to each other, saying an interjection each time you pass the ball. The object is not to get stuck for an interjection and not to repeat an interjection that has already been used.

You may wish to have the student write the definition of an interjection on an index card to add to his other cards for practice at home.

Day 3: Vocabulary, page 151.

Play "ID Tic Tac Toe", adding the new conjunction and interjection cards from Appendix A.

Day 4: Re-read Grammar Lesson, page 152. Complete Interjections, page 153.

Day 5: Read the story again. The student will write his rough draft, using the instructions and checklist on page 154 to self-edit. Check over his work, making sure that he has stayed strictly with the events of the original story and has correct capitalization, spelling and punctuation.

*Locate a copy of <u>Fantastic! Wow! And Unreal! A Book about Interjections and Conjunctions</u> by Ruth Heller to read together in Day 2 of Lesson 26.

Lesson 26

Story: "King Canute on the Seashore" – James Baldwin
Grammar Lesson: Interjections

Day 1: Spelling Practice, page 155 and Interjection Practice, page 156.

Review the definitions of nouns, pronouns, verbs, adjectives, adverbs, prepositions, conjunctions and interjections. Practice "Yankee Doodle Prepositions."

Day 2: Read <u>Fantastic! Wow! And Unreal! A Book about Interjections and Conjunctions</u> together.

Review the definitions of nouns, pronouns, verbs, adjectives, adverbs, prepositions, conjunctions and interjections. Review the State-of-Being Verbs Chant and "Yankee Doodle Prepositions."

Day 3: The student will begin her final draft today, using page 157. Now she may add her own creative touches to the story. Ideas are in the student workbook. Have the student edit her final story using the checklist provided. Check her story carefully; making sure the basic events stay the same and correcting any mechanical errors. The final story will be re-copied on Day 5.

Day 4: Parts of Speech chart, page 158 and Grammar Review, page 159.

Play "Grammar Tic Tac Toe", "ID Tic Tac Toe", "Kaboom," or "Name That Noun" to review past grammatical concepts, if time.

Day 5: The student will copy over the final version of her story today, with your corrections from Day 3 included. Put the final story in a safe place with her others.

Lesson 27

Story: "The Three Goats Named Bruse" – James Baldwin
Grammar Lesson: Review

Day 1: Introduce "The Three Goats Named Bruse."
Read "The Three Goats Named Bruse," pages 160-161, out loud together and discuss.
Who are the main characters? *(the three goats and the Troll)*
What is the problem or conflict? *(the goats want to cross the bridge to get to the better pasture; the Troll will not let them)*
What is the resolution? *(the goats convince the Troll to wait for the biggest goat to eat; the Troll does not realize that the biggest goat is big enough to defend himself)*
Have the student re-tell the story back to you orally.

Review the definitions of nouns, pronouns, verbs, adjectives, adverbs, prepositions, conjunctions and interjections. Practice the State-of-Being Verbs chant and "Yankee Doodle Prepositions" together.

Day 2: Copywork, page 162.

The student has now learned all 8 parts of speech. Technically, every word in the English language can be identified as one of these parts of speech. However, the student is not yet equipped to identify all of them. For example, articles such as "a", "an" or "the" function as adjectives because they are used to modify nouns, but since they do not obviously "decorate" the nouns, the student will have difficulty identifying them as adjectives. This skill will be learned as he grows older.

Write the following sentence on a piece of paper:

> *They eagerly crossed the high bridge over the waterfall.*

Circle and label each word as you identify it together.
-Have the student find the nouns *(bridge, waterfall)*.
-Have the student find any pronouns *(They)*
-Have the student find the verb (you could ask, "What did they <u>do</u>?" *crossed)*.
-Have the student find any adjectives *(the, high, the)*. *You may wish to explain briefly that since the word "the" is referring to the nouns "bridge" and "waterfall", it qualifies as an adjective. Don't worry if he doesn't comprehend this right now. He will eventually, and he is not required to identify anything this hard in his workbook at this point.*
-Have the student find any adverbs *(eagerly)*.

-Have the student find any prepositions (*over*). Sing through "Yankee Doodle Prepositions" if he has trouble.
-Have the student find any conjunctions (*there aren't any*).
-Have the student find any interjections (*there aren't any*).

When you finish, you should have circled and identified every word in the sentence.

Day 3: Vocabulary, page 163.

Play "Grammar Tic Tac Toe", "ID Tic Tac Toe", "Kaboom," "Jumping Interjections" or "Name That Noun" to review past grammatical concepts.

Day 4: Grammar Review – Types of Sentences, page 164.
Play "Kaboom" to review different sentence types.

Day 5: Read the story again. The student will write his rough draft, using the instructions and checklist on page 165 to self-edit. Check over his work, making sure that he has stayed strictly with the events of the original story and has correct capitalization, spelling and punctuation.

Lesson 28

Story: "The Three Goats Named Bruse" – James Baldwin
Grammar Lesson: Review

Day 1: Spelling Practice, page 166 and Crossword, page 167.

Review the definitions of nouns, pronouns, verbs, adjectives, adverbs, prepositions, conjunctions and interjections. Practice "Yankee Doodle Prepositions."

Day 2: Choose a fable from Squids Will Be Squids to read together. Discuss: Who are the main characters? What is the main problem/conflict? How is it solved? What is the moral? What can we learn from this story?

Choose a sentence from the fable you read and write it down. You may wish to use this sentence for copywork or dictation practice. Then practice circling and identifying each word just as in the last lesson.

Day 3: The student will begin her final draft today, using page 168. Now is the time she may add her own creative touches to the story. Ideas are in the student workbook. Have the student edit her final story using the checklist provided. Check her story carefully; making sure the basic events stay the same and correcting any mechanical errors. The final story will be re-copied on Day 5.

Day 4: Grammar Review, page 169.

Play "Grammar Tic Tac Toe", "ID Tic Tac Toe", "Kaboom," "Jumping Interjections" or "Name That Noun" to review past grammatical concepts.

Day 5: The student will copy over the final version of her story today, with your corrections from Day 3 included. Put the final story in a safe place with her others.

Lesson 29

Story: "The Story of William Tell" – James Baldwin
Grammar Lesson: Review

Day 1: Introduce "The Story of William Tell."

Read "The Story of William Tell," pages 170-171, out loud together and discuss.
Who are the main characters? *(the tyrant Gessler, William Tell, William Tell's son)*
What is the problem or conflict? *(Tell laughs at Gessler's ridiculous order that he should bow down to his hat; Gessler orders Tell to shoot an apple off of his son's head as punishment)*
What is the resolution? *(Tell shoots the apple without hurting his son; later Tell shoots Gessler and frees his country)*
Have the student re-tell the story back to you orally.

Review the definitions of nouns, pronouns, verbs, adjectives, adverbs, prepositions, conjunctions and interjections. Practice the State-of-Being Verbs chant and "Yankee Doodle Prepositions" together.

Day 2: Copywork, page 172.

Day 3: Vocabulary, page 173.

Play "Grammar Tic Tac Toe", "ID Tic Tac Toe", "Kaboom," "Jumping Interjections" or "Name That Noun" to review past grammatical concepts.

Day 4: Quotation Review, page 174.
Play "Kaboom" to review different sentence types.

Day 5: Read the story again. The student will write his rough draft, using the instructions and checklist on page 175 to self-edit. Check over his work, making sure that he has stayed strictly with the events of the original story and has correct capitalization, spelling and punctuation.

Lesson 30

Story: "The Story of William Tell" – James Baldwin
Grammar Lesson: Review

Day 1: Spelling Practice, page 176.

Choose a fable from <u>Fables</u> by Arnold Lobel to read together. Discuss: Who are the main characters? What is the main problem/conflict? How is it solved? What is the moral? What can we learn from this story?

Day 2: Grammar Review, pages 177-178.

Day 3: The student will begin her final draft today, using page 179. Now she may add her own creative touches to the story. Ideas are in the student workbook. Have the student edit her final story using the checklist provided. Check her story carefully; making sure the basic events stay the same and correcting any mechanical errors. The final story will be re-copied on Day 4.

Day 4: The student will copy over the final version of her story today, with your corrections from Day 3 included. Put the final story in a safe place with her others.

Day 5: Publish a book of stories, written by your student! Have your child design the cover today and come up with a title for her book. Combine the cover and her finished stories. She may also want to create some illustrations for her favorite ones. Keep the finished product in a three-ring binder, or you may take it to a copy center and ask them to put on a spiral binding for a nominal fee. Either way, your child will have a book that *she* wrote to keep and cherish forever.

Co-operative Lesson Plans

Lesson 1

Story: "The Crow and the Pitcher" – Aesop [e'sop]
Grammar Lesson: Three Requirements for a Sentence.

Class-Time: Introduce "The Crow and the Pitcher." Tell the students about Aesop.

According to ancient historians, Aesop was born as a Greek slave in the area of Samos around 620 B.C. Legend has it that he was born deformed in body, but with a brilliant mind. It is said that his second master eventually freed him because of his obvious wisdom and talent. It is also reported that the citizens of Delphi were so insulted by his keen sarcasm and wit in 564 B.C. that they sentenced him to death and pushed him off a cliff. Hundreds of fables are attributed to Aesop today.

Read "The Crow and the Pitcher," page 1, out loud with the students.
Discuss the story.
Who are the main characters? *(the Crow)*
What is the problem or conflict? *(he can't reach the water in the bottom of the Pitcher)*
What is the resolution? *(the Crow fills the Pitcher with pebbles one by one to raise the water up to his level)*
Have the students re-tell the story orally back to you.

Practice sequencing the events in the story by using the sentence strips found in Appendix A. Make a copy of the sentence strips, cut them apart, and hand out one to each student. Then instruct the students to line up in the correct story order according to their sentence strips. Or you may choose to give each student a copy of all of the sentence strips, cut up, and give them three or four minutes to sequence them by themselves. They may then take the sentence strips home to practice with during the week.

Introduce the Grammar Lesson, page 4.
The students will learn three ways to identify a sentence.

<<1. *A sentence starts with a capital letter and ends with a punctuation mark.*

   Sentences ALWAYS start with capital letters! Sentences will ALWAYS end with either a period, question mark, or exclamation point.
                     .   ?   !
2. *A sentence expresses a complete thought.*

   Sentences are nice! They will never leave you wondering what they're talking about.
3. *A sentence tells us WHO or WHAT, and WHAT THEY DID.*

A sentence will always have a <u>subject</u>, which tells us WHO or WHAT the sentence is about. Also, a sentence will always have a <u>verb</u>, which tells us what the subject did.>>

Practice identifying sentences with the students. You may use the sentence strips from the ordering activity. Change some of them so they are NOT sentences, and ask the children to identify the ones that are sentences, and why or why not.

Discuss the rough drafts the students will be writing this week. They are to re-tell the original story in their own words. Creative touches are not allowed until the final draft is written next week. This week they must stick with the original characters and events exactly as they happened. Rough drafts, if handwritten, should be written in pencil and not pen. Students who have difficulty with the fine motor skill of handwriting may dictate their stories to their mothers at home, at the parent's or teacher's discretion. I would suggest the following accommodation: Final drafts may be dictated completely; rough drafts should be at least partially handwritten. Have them write the first two sentences by themselves, for example, and then they may dictate the rest of the story. Gradually increase the amount of handwriting done by the student.

The students may begin their rough drafts if time permits.

Homework:
Day 1: Copywork, page 2.
Day 2: Vocabulary, page 3.
Day 3: Read Grammar Lesson, page 4. Sentence Practice, pages 5 and 6.
Day 4: Read the story again. Write the rough draft, using the instructions and the checklist on page 7 to self-edit.

Lesson 2

Story: "The Crow and the Pitcher" – Aesop
Grammar Lesson: Three Requirements for a Sentence.

Class-Time: Begin by reading the students a fable of your choice from <u>Fables</u> by Arnold Lobel. Discuss the story with the students. Who were the main characters? What was the problem or conflict? What was the resolution? What does this fable teach us?

Ask one or two students to share their rough drafts with the class. Offer only positive comments in front of the other students. Later, collect the rough drafts and mark suggestions for changes before handing them back at the end of the day.

Review the three requirements for sentences.

Have the students open their books to "The Crow and the Pitcher." Work through the story together, looking at each sentence. Have the students circle the capital letter at the beginning of each sentence with a green crayon or pencil for "go." Have the students circle the end punctuation of each sentence with a red crayon or pencil for "stop."

Students may begin their final drafts if time permits.

Homework:
Day 1: Spelling Practice, page 8 and Grammar Lesson - Sentences, page 9.
Day 2: Write the final draft using page 10. As discussed before, now the students may add a few creative touches to personalize their stories. Characters may be given names, for example. Different animals or people may be used. Students will use provided checklists to self-edit. Additionally, have the parent check these versions today to make sure the basic story stays the same and to correct any spelling or grammatical errors. The final story will be re-copied on Day 4.
Day 3: More Sentence Practice, page 11.
Day 4: The students will copy over the final version of their stories. You may wish to ask the parents to bring in two copies to class; one for you to check and return, and one for you to save. At the end of the year, "publish" a book of your student's stories!

Lesson 3

Story: "The Town Mouse and the Country Mouse" – Aesop
Grammar Lesson: Four Kinds of Sentences.

Class-Time: Introduce "The Town Mouse and the Country Mouse," page 13. Read the story out loud with the students and discuss.
Who are the main characters? *(the Town Mouse and the Country Mouse)*
What is the problem or conflict? *(the Town Mouse does not like the Country Mouse's home; the Country Mouse does not like the dogs at the Town Mouse's home)*
What is the resolution? *(they decide they are each better off in their own homes and learn to be grateful for what they have)*

Have the students re-tell the story back to you orally.

Practice sequencing the events in the story by using the sentence strips from Appendix A. See Lesson 1 for suggestions.

Introduce the Grammar Lesson using page 16.
The students will learn four types of sentences.

<< *There are <u>four</u> different types of sentences.*
1. Statement – declares a fact. Statements usually end with periods.
    Now you must know that a Town Mouse once upon a time went on a visit to his cousin in the country.
2. Question – asks for information. Questions end with a question mark.
    "What is that?"
3. Command – gives an order. Commands usually end with periods, but strong commands could end with exclamation points.
    "Come you with me and I will show you how to live."
4. Exclamation – exclaims; shows emotion. Exclamations usually end with exclamation points.
    "Only!" or "What!" >>

Play a game to practice identifying different types of sentences. Get four index cards. On one write "STATEMENT." On the next write "QUESTION." On the third write "COMMAND" and on the last write "EXCLAMATION." Tape one card to each wall of the classroom. Read aloud the following sentences to the class. The students must decide together what type of sentence you have read and run to the correct wall. For example, if you read a statement, they must run to the wall with the "STATEMENT" card on it.

1. A Town Mouse once upon a time went on a visit. (S)
2. Did he visit his cousin in the country? (Q)
3. Wow! (E)
4. The Country Mouse made him heartily welcome. (S)
5. Yum! (E)
6. Did he offer his cousin food to eat? (Q)
7. Why didn't the Town Mouse like the food in the country? (Q)
8. Come with me. (C)
9. I will show you how to live. (S)
10. Set off for town at once. (C)
11. Suddenly they heard growling and barking. (S)

You may continue the game, making up your own sentences as you go. Save the cards for later use.

Choose two or three students to read their finished stories from last week, if time permits.

Homework:
Day 1: Copywork, page 14.
Day 2: Vocabulary, page 15.
Day 3: Read Grammar Lesson, page 16. Kinds of Sentences, page 17.
Day 4: Read the story again. Write the rough draft, using instructions and checklist on page 18 to self-edit.

Lesson 4

Story: "The Town Mouse and the Country Mouse" – Aesop
Grammar Lesson: Four Kinds of Sentences.

Class-Time: Begin by reading the students a fable of your choice from Fables by Arnold Lobel. Discuss the story with the students. Who were the main characters? What was the problem or conflict? What was the resolution? What does this fable teach us?

Ask one or two students to share their rough drafts with the class. Later, collect the rough drafts and mark suggestions for changes before handing them back at the end of the day.

Review the four types of sentences. Using the index cards from the last lesson, play the same game with sentences you choose from the Fable read aloud earlier.

Homework:
Day 1: Spelling Practice, page 19 and Grammar Lesson Review, page 20.
Day 2: Write the final draft using page 21. As discussed before, now the students may add a few creative touches to personalize their stories. Characters may be given names, for example. Different animals or people may be used. Students will use provided checklists to self-edit. Additionally, have the parent check these versions today to make sure the basic story stays the same and to correct any spelling or grammatical errors. The final story will be re-copied on Day 4.
Day 3: Four Kinds of Sentences, page 22.
Day 4: The students will copy over the final version of their stories. You may wish to ask the parents to bring in two copies to class; one for you to check and return, and one for you to save.

Lesson 5

Story: "Androcles" [an'dr*uc*-klez] – Aesop
Grammar Lesson: Four Rules of Capitalization

Class-Time: Introduce "Androcles," page 23. Read the story out loud with the students and discuss.
Who are the main characters? *(Androcles, the Lion, and the Emperor)*
What is the problem or conflict? *(Androcles is an escaped slave; the Lion has a thorn in his paw; Androcles is later sentenced to be eaten by the Lion)*
What is the resolution? *(Androcles pulls the thorn out of the Lion's paw, thus creating a lifelong friendship; later the Lion refuses to eat Androcles; after hearing the story the Emperor decides to set Androcles free)*
Have the students re-tell the story back to you orally.

Practice sequencing the events in the story by using the sentence strips from Appendix A. See Lesson 1 for suggestions.

Introduce the Grammar Lesson using page 26.
The students will learn four rules for capitalization.

<< 1. *Sentences* start with a capital letter.
   We've already learned about this rule!
2. *Titles* begin with capital letters.
   Titles like Mr., Mrs., Miss, or Dr. always start with capital letters. The important words in book, movie, story or song titles always start with capital letters. For example, our stories, "Androcles" or "The Town Mouse and the Country Mouse."
3. *Proper Names* begin with capital letters.
   Specific names of people, places or things always start with capital letters, because we want to recognize that they are special and unique. For example, the city of Boston is special and unique, so we capitalize the "B". Kristen, Timothy and Melissa are all special and unique people, so we begin their names with capital letters. And the Frisbee is a very special and unique toy, so its name starts with a capital letter too!
4. *The word "I" is always capitalized.*
   Are you special and unique? Of course you are! Then always capitalize the word "I"! >>

Play "KA-BOOM" to review four different kinds of sentences.
   Set-up: Copy the "Ka-Boom" pages from Appendix A. You may wish to copy them on cardstock for durability. For additional durability, "laminate" them with clear shelf paper. Put the strips in an empty, clean potato chip can. Paste a piece of colorful paper around the barrel of the can and write "Ka-boom!" on it.

Play: Students draw strips out of the can one at a time. If they choose a sentence, they must tell you what kind of sentence it is. If they are correct, they keep the sentence strip. If incorrect, they must put it back in the can. If they draw "Ka-boom!" they must put all of their strips back in the can. The student with the most strips at the end of the game wins.

Choose two or three students to read their finished stories from last week, if time permits.

Homework:
Day 1: Copywork, page 24.
Day 2: Vocabulary, page 25.
Day 3: Read Grammar Lesson, page 26. Capitalization Practice, pages 27-28.
Day 4: Read the story again. Write the rough draft, using instructions and checklist on page 29 to self-edit.

Lesson 6

Story: "Androcles" – Aesop
Grammar Lesson: Four Rules of Capitalization

Class-Time: Begin by reading the students a fable of your choice from Fables by Arnold Lobel. Discuss the story with the students. Who were the main characters? What was the problem or conflict? What was the resolution? What does this fable teach us?

Ask one or two students to share their rough drafts with the class. Later, collect the rough drafts and mark suggestions for changes before handing them back at the end of the day.

Use "The Town Mouse and the Country Mouse", page 13 in the students' workbooks, to practice capitalization rules. Each student will need four crayons or colored pencils: green, blue, red and yellow. Work through the story together, circling all the capital letters with the following instructions:
    1. Circle the letter in green if the letter is at the beginning of a sentence.
    2. Circle the letter in blue if it is at the beginning of a name.
    3. Circle the letter in red if it is at the beginning of a title.
    4. Circle the letter in yellow if it is the word "I."

Play "Kaboom" if you have time to review the 4 types of sentences. Variation: Review the capitalization rules by indicating a capital letter on the sentence the student has chosen and asking for the reason why it is capitalized.

Homework:
Day 1: Spelling Practice, page 30 and Capitalization, page 31.
Day 2: Write the final draft using page 32. As discussed before, now the students may add a few creative touches to personalize their stories. Characters may be given names, for example. Different animals or people may be used. Students will use provided checklists to self-edit. Additionally, have the parent check these versions today to make sure the basic story stays the same and to correct any spelling or grammatical errors. The final story will be re-copied on Day 4.
Day 3: Capitalization Review, page 33.
Day 4: The students will copy over the final version of their stories. You may wish to ask the parents to bring in two copies to class; one for you to check and return, and one for you to save.

Lesson 7

Story: "Julius Caesar [se'*zur*]" – James Baldwin
Grammar Lesson: Punctuation Traffic Signals

Class-Time: Introduce "Julius Caesar." Give some background information on the author, James Baldwin.

James Baldwin was born in Indiana in 1841 and lived until 1925. His childhood was marked by infrequent schooling and a limited access to books. Still, his father had a "library" that consisted of two shelves of books. These books were precious to James, and developed a love of literature in him that lasted a lifetime. He grew up to become first a teacher, founding and improving many schools in Indiana. During this time he began writing. Some of the books he wrote were for teachers, but most of them were books of stories for children. He loved to re-tell old classics, and by doing this he made exciting moral tales accessible to students all over the country and helped many children develop the same love of reading that he had fostered in himself so many years before. In 1887 Baldwin moved east to join the education department of Harper & Brothers, and later the American Book Company. While editing numerous textbooks, he continued writing. At one time it was said that he had either written or edited at least half of all the textbooks being used in schools across the country!

Read "Julius Caesar," pages 34-35, out loud with the students and discuss.
Who are the main characters? *(Julius Caesar, Caesar's officers, the boat's captain)*

What is the problem or conflict? *(the officers make fun of the village mayor; a storm threatens to capsize Caesar's boat and the captain is frightened)*
What is the resolution? *(Caesar rebukes the officer by saying it is better to be in charge of a small village than to be the second man in command of a large city; Caesar comforts the captain with his bravery in the face of the storm)*
Have the students re-tell the story back to you orally.

Practice sequencing the events in the story by using the sentence strips from Appendix A. See Lesson 1 for suggestions.

Introduce the Grammar Lesson using page 38.
The students will learn Punctuation Traffic Signals.

<< For this grammar lesson, let's think of punctuation as traffic signals in our writing. The punctuation marks tell us when to slow down and when to stop, and help to keep our words from bumping into each other.
The Red Lights: *These are the easy ones, and we've already learned them! Think of the period, the exclamation point, and the question mark as "red lights." When you see them, the sentence stops! Don't start moving again until you see the "green light" of the next sentence's beginning capital letter.*
The Yield Signs: *Commas act like yield signs; they tell you to slow down before proceeding. Take a breath, look around, and then continue on with your journey of reading the sentence.*
The Stop Signs: *Semi-colons act like stop signs. They tell the reader to slow down and stop before continuing on again.>>*

Put the new grammatical concepts into practice by playing "Red Light, Green Light." One player is the Traffic Cop and stands at one end of the room. The other children line up at the other end. The Traffic Cop calls out "Capital Letter!" (instead of "Green Light") when he wants the other players to start moving. The other players walk towards the Traffic Cop. The Traffic Cop can call out "Exclamation Point!" or "Period!" or "Question Mark!" when he wants the other players to stop. He may then start them up again by calling "Capital Letter!" The Traffic Cop may also call out, "Comma!" at which point the students must stop, say "Take a break!" and then continue on. If the Traffic Cop catches anyone not following his instructions, he may send them back to start. The first student to reach the Traffic Cop becomes the next Traffic Cop.

Choose two or three students to read their finished stories from last week, if time permits.

Homework:
Day 1: Copywork, page 36.
Day 2: Vocabulary, page 37.
Day 3: Read Grammar Lesson, page 38. Punctuation Practice, page 39.
Day 4: Read the story again. Write the rough draft, using instructions and checklist on page 40 to self-edit.

Lesson 8

Story: "Julius Caesar" – James Baldwin
Grammar Lesson: Punctuation Traffic Signals

Class-Time: Ask one or two students to share their rough drafts with the class. Later, collect the rough drafts and mark suggestions for changes before handing them back at the end of the day.

Read Punctuation Takes a Vacation by Robin Pulver. Discuss the story with the students. What happened when the punctuation marks left for vacation? Did the words that were left behind know how to behave?

Play "Red Light, Green Light" again to review the concepts of punctuation.

Play "Kaboom" if you have time to review the 4 types of sentences. Variation: Review the punctuation rules by indicating a punctuation mark on the sentence that the student has chosen and asking for the "movement" that the "traffic signal" tells; i.e., stop, pause, stop and then move on.

Homework:
Day 1: Spelling Practice, page 41 and Punctuation Review, page 42.
Day 2: Write the final draft using page 43. Creative touches this week must be done very carefully. Read the student workbook page for details and suggestions. Students will use provided checklists to self-edit. Additionally, have the parent check these versions today to make sure the basic story stays the same and to correct any spelling or grammatical errors. The final story will be re-copied on Day 4.
Day 3: Will the Real Punctuation Please Stand Up?, pages 44-45.
Day 4: The students will copy over the final version of their stories. You may wish to ask the parents to bring in two copies to class; one for you to check and return, and one for you to save.

Lesson 9

Story: "The Princess and the Pea" – Hans Christian Andersen
Grammar Lesson: Simple Quotes: Direct vs. Indirect and Punctuation

Class-Time: Introduce "The Princess and the Pea." Give some background information on the author, Hans Christian Andersen.

Hans Christian Andersen was born in 1805 in the slums of Odense, Denmark. His mother was a washerwoman and his father a poor shoemaker. Andersen had very little education until he was older, but when he was a young boy his father, who loved literature, did much to encourage Andersen's love of stories and fairy tales. He took him to see plays, encouraged him to make up stories, and read to him, often from "Arabian Nights." After a failed attempt at a dramatic career, Andersen was granted tuition to a local grammar school (where he studied with 11 year olds even though he was 17!) and then later to Copenhagen University. He became a successful writer and poet. His most famous book has always been "Fairy Tales and Stories." In a time when other writers made their fortune by re-writing old folk tales, only 12 of Andersen's 156 fairy tales were not original.

Read "The Princess and the Pea," pages 46-47, out loud with the students and discuss.
Who are the main characters? *(the prince, the princess, the old queen)*
What is the problem or conflict? *(the prince needs to marry a princess but he has difficulty finding a real one)*
What is the resolution? *(the queen puts a pea underneath the princess' mattresses as a test to see if she is a genuine princess)*
Have the students re-tell the story back to you orally.

Practice sequencing the events in the story by using the sentence strips from Appendix A. See Lesson 1 for suggestions.

Introduce the Grammar Lesson using pages 50-51.
The students will learn about Simple Quotes.

<< When we talk about quotes in a story, we are talking about words that people are saying.
Direct Quotes *are words that the character is actually saying, and are always surrounded by quotation marks.*
    Example: "Ouch!" cried the princess.
Indirect Quotes *are words that the storyteller tells us were said by the characters. They do not have quotation marks.*

Example: The princess cried out in pain. or The princess said that she did not sleep well the night before.

Indirect quotes are easy to punctuate; use the same rules we learned for regular sentences. Begin with a capital letter, use commas if you want the reader to pause, semi-colons if you want the reader to stop and then continue on, and always end with a period, exclamation point or question mark.
Direct quotes can be more difficult to punctuate.
-The words actually said by a character must be surrounded by quotation marks.
>*"I don't think this bed is very comfortable."*
-The words inside the quotation marks will always start with a beginning capital letter, just like a sentence.
-If the narrator introduces the quote (She said, "Ouch!"), there will be a comma before the quotation marks, because you want the reader to pause before reading the quote, and end punctuation at the end <u>*inside the quotation marks*</u> *to show that the sentence is finished.*
>*He asked, "Why didn't you sleep well?"*
-If the narrator finishes the quote instead ("Ouch," she said.) AND the quote from the character was a sentence that should end in a period, then a comma is put at the end of the quote, inside the quotation marks, so that there will be a pause before finishing the sentence, and the end punctuation will be put at the end, after the narrator concludes the sentence.
>*"I need more mattresses," said the queen.*
-If the character says in a direct quote something that would end with an exclamation point or a question mark, these are left in the quote, and the sentence will still end with an end punctuation mark after the narrator finishes it.
>*"Why didn't you sleep well?" he asked.*
>*"Goodness gracious!" she cried. >>*

Please note – this is a rather difficult grammar lesson! Concentrate on teaching the students to distinguish between direct and indirect quotes. Punctuation within quotes may be corrected as needed in the students' stories throughout the year and will be mastered gradually.

Put the new grammatical concepts into practice by playing a new version of "Kaboom", using the "Simple Quotes" sentence strips in Appendix A. Copy these strips on a different color paper from the first set of sentences so you have two sets to play with – the first set for identifying kinds of sentences, the second set for identifying kinds of quotes. Play with the second set of sentences today. Students will draw a sentence strip and tell you whether the sentence contains a direct quote or an indirect quote. As before, if they are right, they may keep the strip. If they draw "Kaboom!", they must put all of their strips back in the can.

Choose two or three students to read their finished stories from last week, if time permits.

Homework:
Day 1: Copywork, page 48.
Day 2: Vocabulary, page 49.
Day 3: Read Grammar Lesson, pages 50-51. Quotations, page 52.
Day 4: Read the story again. Write the rough draft, using instructions and checklist on page 53 to self-edit.

Lesson 10

Story: "The Princess and the Pea," Hans Christian Andersen
Grammar Lesson: Simple Quotes: Direct vs. Indirect and Punctuation

Class-Time: Ask one or two students to share their rough drafts with the class. Later, collect the rough drafts and mark suggestions for changes before handing them back at the end of the day.

Choose a fable from Squids Will Be Squids by John Scieszka to read together. Discuss: what is the moral? What can we learn from this story? These stories are wonderful, and short, so you may decide to read two or three.

Play "Kaboom" again with the second set of sentences to review Direct vs. Indirect Quotes. Variation: if your students seem to be grasping the concept easily, have them not only identify the kind of quote, but also change the sentence from a direct to an indirect quote or vice versa.

Play "Red Light, Green Light" if you have time to review Punctuation Traffic Signals.

Homework:
Day 1: Spelling Practice, page 54 and Practice with Simple Quotes, page 55.
Day 2: Write the final draft using page 56. Ideas for creative touches are in the student workbook. Students will use provided checklists to self-edit. Additionally, have the parent check these versions today to make sure the basic story stays the same and to correct any spelling or grammatical errors. The final story will be re-copied on Day 4.
Day 3: Quotations, pages 57-58 and Grammar Review, page 59.

Day 4: The students will copy over the final version of their stories. You may wish to ask the parents to bring in two copies to class; one for you to check and return, and one for you to save.

Lesson 11

Story: "The Elves and the Shoemaker" – Horace E. Scudder
Grammar Lesson: Nouns

Class-Time: Introduce "The Elves and the Shoemaker." Give some background information on the author, Horace E. Scudder.

Horace E. Scudder (1838-1902) was a very popular children's author of the nineteenth century. His most popular books were <u>The Book of Fables</u>, <u>The Book of Folk Stores</u>, <u>The Book of Legends</u> and <u>Fables and Folk Stories</u>. He worked hard to have good literature introduced into schools. To this end, he wrote numerous historical and biographical works, including a biography of George Washington that is still considered to be the finest ever written for children.

Read "The Elves and the Shoemaker," pages 60-61, out loud with the students and discuss.
Who are the main characters? *(the Shoemaker and his wife, the Elves*
What is the problem or conflict? *(the Shoemaker is running out of money)*
What is the resolution? *(the Elves make beautiful shoes for the Shoemaker to sell; the Shoemaker's wife makes clothes for the Elves to say thank you)*
Have the students re-tell the story back to you orally.

Hand out copies of the "Storyboard" page from Appendix A. Read the story one more time and have the children draw simple pictures of the events as they happen.

Introduce the Grammar Lesson using page 64.
The students will learn about Nouns.

<< A <u>noun</u> is the name of a person, place, thing, or idea.
Examples:
People – elves, shoemaker, customer, wife
Places – shop, village, workroom, street
Things – shoe, leather, stitch, curtain, bench
Ideas – honesty, love, hope, wonder, troubles
Most nouns are called Common Nouns. Nouns that name specific people or places are called Proper Nouns. Proper Nouns always start with capital letters.
Example: Sally, John, Mr. Jones, Seattle, Boston >>

This is a fairly easy grammar lesson. The hardest part of learning nouns is to grasp the concept of nouns as names of ideas. Pay special attention to this, but don't get stuck on it if they have trouble. This idea will sink in as the students get older and can better comprehend abstract concepts such as *hope, love, honesty,* or *fate.*

Put the new grammatical concepts into practice by playing "Name That Noun." Copy and hand out the game page from Appendix A. Play with one column at a time. The first round will be "Persons". Give the students two minutes to write down as many nouns for "persons" that they can think of. You may either play to see how many each student can come up with, or have the students compare their lists, cross out the duplicates, and only score points for the original nouns. Play again with "Places," "Things," and "Ideas."

Choose two or three students to read their finished stories from last week, if time permits.

Homework:
Day 1: Copywork, page 62.
Day 2: Vocabulary, page 63.
Day 3: Read Grammar Lesson, page 64. Nouns, page 65.
Day 4: Read the story again. Write the rough draft, using instructions and checklist on page 66 to self-edit.

Lesson 12

Story: "The Elves and the Shoemaker," by Horace E. Scudder
Grammar Lesson: Nouns

Class-Time: Ask one or two students to share their rough drafts with the class. Later, collect the rough drafts and mark suggestions for changes before handing them back at the end of the day.

Choose a fable from Fables by Arnold Lobel to read together. Discuss: Who are the main characters? What is the main problem/conflict? How is it solved? What is the moral? What can we learn from this story?

Go through "The Elves and the Shoemaker" together in the workbooks, circling all the nouns in purple. You may also choose to review past concepts by circling beginning capital letters in green, end punctuation in red, and quotation marks, commas and semi-colons in blue.

Play another round of "Name That Noun," OR "Kaboom!" OR "Red Light, Green Light."

Homework:
Day 1: Spelling Practice, page 67 and Noun Practice, page 68.
Day 2: Write the final draft using page 69. Ideas for creative touches are in the student workbook. Students will use provided checklists to self-edit. Additionally, have the parent check these versions today to make sure the basic story stays the same and to correct any spelling or grammatical errors. The final story will be re-copied on Day 4.
Day 3: Parts of Speech chart, page 70 and Grammar Review, pages 71-72.
Day 4: The students will copy over the final version of their stories. You may wish to ask the parents to bring in two copies to class; one for you to check and return, and one for you to save.

Lesson 13

Story: "The Cat, the Monkey and the Chestnuts" – Horace E. Scudder
Grammar Lesson: Pronouns

Class-Time: Introduce "The Cat, the Monkey and the Chestnuts."
Read "The Cat, the Monkey and the Chestnuts," page 73, out loud with the students and discuss.
Who are the main characters? *(the Cat and the Monkey)*
What is the problem or conflict? *(they want to get the chestnuts out of the hot ashes to eat them)*
What is the resolution? *(the Monkey flatters the Cat into getting the chestnuts out of the hot ashes, the Monkey eats them while the Cat is getting them out)*
Have the students re-tell the story back to you orally.

Hand out copies of the "Storyboard" page from Appendix A. Read the story one more time, having the children draw simple pictures of the events as they happen.

Introduce the Grammar Lesson using page 76.
The students will learn about Pronouns.

*<< A **pronoun** is a word that takes the place of a noun.*
Examples: I, you, he, she, it, we, they, my, mine, me, our,
*   them*
In the title of our story, there are three nouns:
*   "The **Cat**, the **Monkey,** and the **Chestnuts**"*

If we replaced each noun with a pronoun, our silly title would look like this:
*"**She, He**, and **Them**"*
It's a good thing we have nouns, so we know what we are talking about! Pronouns are important too; they keep our writing from sounding awkward.
Look at this sentence from our story, with all nouns and no pronouns:
Scarcely had the Cat touched the hot ashes than the Cat drew back with a cry, for the Cat had burned the Cat's paw.
Now here it is again, with pronouns put back in:
Scarcely had the Cat touched the hot ashes than <u>she</u> drew back with a cry, for <u>she</u> had burned <u>her</u> paw.
It sounds much better! >>

Review the definition of a noun and practice the definition of a pronoun. You may choose to have the students write the definitions on index cards to practice with at home.

Put the new grammatical concepts into practice by playing "ID Tic Tac Toe." Copy the word page (Nouns and Pronouns) from Appendix A onto stiff card stock, cut into word squares and put into a bag. Divide students into two teams: Xs and Os. Alternate turns between the players of the two teams. On his turn, the player will pull one word square from the bag and must identify it as either a noun or a pronoun. If he is correct, he may place an X or an O for his team onto a tic tac toe board. If he is incorrect, he forfeits his turn.

Choose two or three students to read their finished stories from last week, if time permits.

Homework:
Day 1: Copywork, page 74.
Day 2: Vocabulary, page 75.
Day 3: Read Grammar Lesson, page 76. Pronouns, page 77.
Day 4: Read the story again. Write the rough draft, using instructions and checklist on page 78 to self-edit.

Lesson 14

Story: "The Cat, the Monkey and the Chestnuts," by Horace E. Scudder
Grammar Lesson: Pronouns

Class-Time: Ask one or two students to share their rough drafts with the class. Later, collect the rough drafts and mark suggestions for changes before handing them back at the end of the day.

Choose a fable from <u>Squids Will Be Squids</u> to read together. Discuss: Who are the main characters? What is the main problem/conflict? How is it solved? What is the moral? What can we learn from this story?

Review the definitions of nouns and pronouns. Work on getting the students to memorize them. You may put the definition to a silly rhythm and then march around the room together chanting it. You may choose to write the definition on the board, then say it repeatedly, having the students erase one word each time until the class is saying the definition without any words written on the board.

Go through the story together in the workbooks, circling all the nouns in purple and the pronouns in yellow. You may also choose to review past concepts by circling beginning capital letters in green, end punctuation in red, and quotation marks, commas and semi-colons in blue.

Play "Name That Noun," OR "Kaboom!" OR "Red Light, Green Light."

Homework:
Day 1: Spelling Practice, page 79 and Pronoun Practice, page 80.
Day 2: Write the final draft using page 81. Ideas for creative touches are in the student workbook. Students will use provided checklists to self-edit. Additionally, have the parent check these versions today to make sure the basic story stays the same and to correct any spelling or grammatical errors. The final story will be re-copied on Day 4.
Day 3: Parts of Speech chart, page 82 and More Pronouns, page 83.
Day 4: The students will copy over the final version of their stories. You may wish to ask the parents to bring in two copies to class; one for you to check and return, and one for you to save.

Lesson 15

Story: "How the Princess was Beaten in a Race" – Horace E. Scudder
Grammar Lesson: Verbs

Class-Time: Introduce "How the Princess was Beaten in a Race."
Read "How the Princess was Beaten in a Race," pages 84-85, out loud with the students and discuss.
Who are the main characters? *(the princess and the poor young man)*
What is the problem or conflict? *(the young man must beat the princess in a race in order to marry her)*
What is the resolution? *(the young man uses various tricks to distract the princess so that he can beat her in the race)*

Have the students re-tell the story back to you orally.

Practice sequencing the events in the story by using the sentence strips from Appendix A. See Lesson 1 for suggestions.

Review the definitions of nouns and pronouns.

Introduce the Grammar Lesson using page 88.
The students will learn about verbs.

<<*A verb is a word that shows an action or a state of being.*
There are two kinds of verbs we will learn about:
Action Verbs – An action verb is a word that shows an action, like run, walk, eat, think, chew, and study.
Here's an easy test for action verbs: If you can put the word in the sentence, "I can _____,*" and it makes sense, then it is an action verb.*
For example, "I can run." "I can walk." "I can think." "I can study."
State of Being Verbs – A state-of-being verb is a word that states that something IS. For example, "Melissa IS smart." "Timothy IS funny." "Kristen IS beautiful." "He WAS tired." "They WERE in the pool." "I AM happy."
You can remember the eight state-of-being verbs with a little chant. The rhythm goes like this: slow, slow, quick-quick, slow, slow, slow, slow.
Now add the following words: is, am, were-was, are, be, being, been. >>

Practice the State-of-Being Verbs chant together. An audio file of this chant can be found at :
http://www.kyrene.k12.az.us/schools/brisas/sunda/verb/verbs.wav
The chant is sung like this, in a singsong voice:

"is,	am,	were - was - are,	be,	being,	been."
slow,	*slow,*	*quick – quick - slow, slow,*	*slow,*	*slow.*	
clap,	*clap,*	*clap - clap - clap, clap,*	*clap,*	*clap.*	

You may wish to have the students write the definition of a verb on an index card to add to their other cards for practice at home.

Note: For the purposes of this level, we will stick with two simple kinds of action and state-of-being verbs. Helping verbs will be taught in the future.

Practice the concept of action verbs by playing Verb Charades: Help the class brainstorm as many action verbs as possible for three minutes. Write their action verbs on the board. Then illustrate that these verbs show action by playing charades. One student chooses an action verb from the board without telling anyone, and then acts it out while the other students guess which one it is. The student who guesses correctly goes next.

Choose two or three students to read their finished stories from last week.

Homework:
Day 1: Copywork, page 86.
Day 2: Vocabulary, page 87.
Day 3: Read Grammar Lesson, page 88. Verbs, page 89.
Day 4: Read the story again. Write the rough draft, using instructions and checklist on page 90 to self-edit.

Lesson 16

Story: "How the Princess was Beaten in a Race" – Horace E. Scudder
Grammar Lesson: Verbs

Class-Time: Ask one or two students to share their rough drafts with the class. Later, collect the rough drafts and mark suggestions for changes before handing them back at the end of the day.

Review the definitions of nouns, pronouns and verbs. Review the State-of-Being Verbs Chant.

You may choose to play Grammar Tic-Tac-Toe to practice the parts of speech definitions: divide the students into two teams. Alternating teams, each player must give the definition you ask for correctly before placing an X or O on the board. If they are wrong, play forfeits to the other team. Ask the three definitions, noun, pronoun and verb, mixing them up, for one round of the game.

Review the concepts of action and state-of-being verbs by reading the stories of Action Anna and Stanley State-of-Being, found in Appendix A.

Play "Kaboom," or "Name That Noun" to review past grammatical concepts, if time.

Homework:
Day 1: Spelling Practice, page 91 and Verb Practice, page 92.
Day 2: Write the final draft using page 93. Ideas for creative touches are in the student workbook. Students will use provided checklists to self-edit. Additionally, have the parent check these versions today to make sure the basic story stays the same and to correct any spelling or grammatical errors. The final story will be re-copied on Day 4.
Day 3: Parts of Speech chart, page 94 and Grammar Review, page 95.

Day 4: The students will copy over the final versions of their stories. You may wish to ask the parents to bring in two copies to class; one for you to check and return and one for you to save.

Lesson 17

Story: "Cornelia's Jewels" – James Baldwin
Grammar Lesson: Adjectives

Class-Time: Introduce "Cornelia's Jewels."
Read "Cornelia's Jewels," pages 96 and 97, out loud with the students and discuss.
Who are the main characters? *(the two sons, the mother and her friend)*
What is the problem or conflict? *(the boys wish their mother could have fine jewels)*
What is the resolution? *(the mother calls her sons her jewels)*
Have the students re-tell the story back to you orally.

Practice sequencing the events in the story by using the sentence strips from Appendix A. See Lesson 1 for suggestions.

Review the definitions of nouns, pronouns and verbs. Practice the State-of-Being Verbs chant together.

Introduce the Grammar Lesson using page 100.
The students will learn about adjectives.

<< An ***adjective*** is a word that "decorates" a noun or a pronoun.
Adjectives add color to our writing!
Consider the first two sentences of "Cornelia's Jewels". First, let's read them without any adjectives:
> *It was morning in the city of Rome years ago. In a house in a garden, two boys were standing.*

Now let's read them with the adjectives:
> *It was a bright morning in the old city of Rome many hundred years ago. In a vine-covered summer-house in a beautiful garden, two boys were standing.*

Stories are much more interesting when they have adjectives added in. The reader can picture the scene just as the author intended, and will find the story much more enjoyable.>>

You may wish to have the students write the definition of an adjective on an index card to add to their other cards for practice at home.

Practice the concept of adjectives by playing the Necklace Game: Use the five pictures of necklaces from Appendix A. Call one or two students up and secretly show them one necklace picture. Then ask them to describe to the rest of the class their necklace, <u>using only adjectives.</u> The other students will guess which necklace they are describing. Repeat with the other students.

Choose two or three students to read their finished stories from last week, if time permits.

Homework:
Day 1: Copywork, page 98.
Day 2: Vocabulary, page 99.
Day 3: Read Grammar Lesson, page 100. Adjectives, page 101.
Day 4: Read the story again. Write the rough draft, using instructions and checklist on page 102 to self-edit.

Lesson 18

Story: "Cornelia's Jewels" – James Baldwin
Grammar Lesson: Adjectives

Class-Time: Ask one or two students to share their rough drafts with the class. Later, collect the rough drafts and mark suggestions for changes before handing them back at the end of the day.

Choose two or three poems from <u>Where the Sidewalk Ends</u> by Shel Silverstein to read together.

Review the definitions of nouns, pronouns, verbs and adjectives. Review the State-of-Being Verbs Chant.

Play ID Tic Tac Toe with the word cards to practice identifying parts of speech. Add word cards of verbs and adjectives from Appendix A, so the students will be identifying nouns, pronouns, verbs and adjectives in the game.

Play "Kaboom," or "Name That Noun" to review past grammatical concepts, if time.

Homework:
Day 1: Spelling Practice, page 103, and Adjective Practice, page 104.
Day 2: Write the final draft using page 105. Ideas for creative touches are in the student workbook. Students will use provided checklists to self-edit. Additionally, have the parent check these versions today to make sure the basic story stays the same and to correct any spelling or grammatical errors. The final story will be re-copied on Day 4.
Day 3: Parts of Speech chart, page 106 and Grammar Review, page 107.
Day 4: The students will copy over the final versions of their stories. You may wish to ask the parents to bring in two copies to class; one for you to check and return and one for you to save.

Lesson 19

Story: "Alexander and Bucephalus [byOOse′fulus]" – James Baldwin
Grammar Lesson: Adverbs

Class-Time: Introduce "Alexander and Bucephalus."
Read "Alexander and Bucephalus," pages 108-109, out loud with the students and discuss.
Who are the main characters? *(King Philip, Bucephalus, Alexander)*
What is the problem or conflict? *(Bucephalus is a wild horse and will not let any of the king's men ride him)*
What is the resolution? *(Alexander notices that the horse is afraid of his own shadow; he rides him; they become inseparable and Alexander goes on to become Alexander the Great)*
Have the students re-tell the story back to you orally.

Rewrite a simple version of the story together (on a blackboard or whiteboard) using strictly nouns/pronouns and verbs. Then together decide where to "decorate" your story by adding adjectives.

Review the definitions of nouns, pronouns, verbs and adjectives. Practice the State-of-Being Verbs chant together.

Introduce the Grammar Lesson using page 112.
The students will learn about adverbs.

<< *An **adverb** is a word that "decorates" a verb.*
Adverbs also add color to our writing, just like adjectives!
<u>Most</u> *adverbs end in –ly. For example: He ran quickly. She gave money generously.*
Sally jumped easily over the creek. Few don't, such as outside, tomorrow, there, then or

more.
Adverbs answer the questions, "When?" "Where?", "How?" and "How much?"
For example, When did he run? He ran recently.
Where did he run? He ran outside.
How did he run? He ran quickly.
How much did he run? He ran occasionally. >>

You may wish to have the students write the definition of an adverb on an index card to add to their other cards for practice at home.

Play Grammar Tic-Tac-Toe to practice the definitions: divide the students into two teams. Alternating teams, each player must give you one of the definitions correctly before placing an X or O on the board. If they are wrong, play forfeits to the other team. Ask for definitions of nouns, pronouns, verbs, adjectives and adverbs, mixing them up, for one round of the game.

Choose two or three students to read their finished stories from last week, if time permits.

Homework:
Day 1: Copywork, page 110.
Day 2: Vocabulary, page 111.
Day 3: Read Grammar Lesson, page 112. Adverbs, page 113.
Day 4: Read the story again. Write the rough draft, using instructions and checklist on page 114 to self-edit.

Lesson 20

Story: "Alexander and Bucephalus" – James Baldwin
Grammar Lesson: Adverbs

Class-Time: Ask one or two students to share their rough drafts with the class. Later, collect the rough drafts and mark suggestions for changes before handing them back at the end of the day.

Choose a fable from Squids Will Be Squids to read together. Discuss: Who are the main characters? What is the main problem/conflict? How is it solved? What is the moral? What can we learn from this story?

Together, re-write a simple version of the fable on the board, using only nouns/pronouns and verbs. Next, together add adjectives and adverbs to "decorate" the story. If you have a white board, use a different color marker to add the "decorating words."

Review the definitions of nouns, pronouns, verbs, adjectives and adverbs. Review the State-of-Being Verbs Chant.

Play "Grammar Tic Tac Toe", "ID Tic Tac Toe", "Kaboom," or "Name That Noun" to review past grammatical concepts, if time.

Homework:
Day 1: Spelling Practice, page 115 and Adverb Practice, page 116.
Day 2: Write the final draft using page 117. Ideas for creative touches are in the student workbook. Students will use provided checklists to self-edit. Additionally, have the parent check these versions today to make sure the basic story stays the same and to correct any spelling or grammatical errors. The final story will be re-copied on Day 4.
Day 3: Parts of Speech chart, page 118 and Grammar Review, pages 119-120.
Day 4: The students will copy over the final versions of their stories. You may wish to ask the parents to bring in two copies to class; one for you to check and return and one for you to save.

Lesson 21

Story: "King Alfred and the Cakes" – James Baldwin
Grammar Lesson: Prepositions

Class-Time: Introduce "King Alfred and the Cakes."
Read "King Alfred and the Cakes," pages 121-122, out loud with the students and discuss.
Who are the main characters? *(King Alfred, the woodcutter's wife)*
What is the problem or conflict? *(the King is so distracted by fighting the Danes that he forgets to watch the cakes; they burn)*
What is the resolution? *(the woodcutter's wife scolds the King; the King is amused at being scolded by her; he goes on to beat the Danes in a great battle)*
Have the students re-tell the story back to you orally.

Review the definitions of nouns, pronouns, verbs, adjectives and adverbs. Practice the State-of-Being Verbs chant together.

Introduce the Grammar Lesson using page 125.
The students will learn about prepositions.

<< A *preposition* is a word that relates a noun or pronoun to other words in a sentence. An easy way to identify a preposition is to ask if the word is something a squirrel can do to a tree! For example, the squirrel can go near the tree, around the tree, over the tree, beside the tree, through the tree (imagine the tree is hollow) and under the tree.

Memorize this song to the tune of "Yankee Doodle". It will help you remember 28 different prepositions.

Yankee Doodle Prepositions
Above, across, after, around,
And then comes at;
Before, behind, below, beside,
Between and by.
Down and during, for and from,
In, inside and into;
Of, off, on, out, over, through,
To, under, up and with! >>

Demonstrate the concept of "what a squirrel can do to a tree" with a stuffed animal. Brainstorm! Ask the students, "What can a squirrel do to a tree?" and write their answers down.

You may wish to have the students write the definition of a preposition on an index card to add to their other cards for practice at home.

Play ID Tic-Tac-Toe to practice identifying different parts of speech. Add the adverb and preposition cards from Appendix A to the game.

Choose two or three students to read their finished stories from last week, if time permits.

Homework:
Practice "Yankee Doodle Prepositions" each day.
Day 1: Copywork, page 123.
Day 2: Vocabulary, page 124.
Day 3: Read Grammar Lesson, page 125. Prepositions, page 126.
Day 4: Read the story again. Write the rough draft, using instructions and checklist on page 127 to self-edit.

Lesson 22

Story: "King Alfred and the Cakes" – James Baldwin
Grammar Lesson: Prepositions

Class-Time: Ask one or two students to share their rough drafts with the class. Later, collect the rough drafts and mark suggestions for changes before handing them back at the end of the day.

Choose two or three poems from <u>Where the Sidewalk Ends</u> by Shel Silverstein to read together.

Review the definitions of nouns, pronouns, verbs, adjectives, adverbs and prepositions. Review the State-of-Being Verbs Chant.

Do "King Alfred and the Cakes Fun with Parts of Speech" activity together from Appendix A.

Play "Grammar Tic Tac Toe", "ID Tic Tac Toe", "Kaboom," or "Name That Noun" to review past grammatical concepts, if time.

Homework:
Practice "Yankee Doodle Prepositions" each day.
Day 1: Spelling Practice, page 128 and Preposition Practice, page 129.
Day 2: Write the final draft using page 130. Ideas for creative touches are in the student workbook. Students will use provided checklists to self-edit. Additionally, have the parent check these versions today to make sure the basic story stays the same and to correct any spelling or grammatical errors. The final story will be re-copied on Day 4.
Day 3: Parts of Speech chart, page 131 and Grammar Review, pages 132-133.
Day 4: The students will copy over the final versions of their stories. You may wish to ask the parents to bring in two copies to class; one for you to check and return and one for you to save.

Lesson 23

Story: "The Travels of Ching" – Robert Bright
Grammar Lesson: Conjunctions

Class-Time: Introduce "The Travels of Ching."

Robert Bright (1902-1988) was a popular children's author of the twentieth century. He wrote the popular "Georgie" books among others.

Read "The Travels of Ching," pages 134-136, out loud with the students and discuss.
Who are the main characters? *(Ching and the little girl)*
What is the problem or conflict? *(the little girl cannot afford to buy Ching; Ching cannot find a home)*
What is the resolution? *(the little girl's uncle in America buys Ching and sends him to his niece in China…the same little girl; the little girl and Ching are finally happy together)*
Look at a globe or a map to see just how far Ching traveled before he found his home.
Have the students re-tell the story back to you orally.
Use the sentence strips from Appendix A to practice sequencing the events of the story.

Review the definitions of nouns, pronouns, verbs, adjectives, adverbs and prepositions. Practice the State-of-Being Verbs chant and "Yankee Doodle Prepositions."

Introduce the Grammar Lesson using page 139.
The students will learn about conjunctions.

*<< A **conjunction** is a joining word that connects words or phrases together.*
The most popular conjunction is the word "and."
"And" is as powerful as super-glue!
It can connect words, like "bat and ball," "milk and cookies," or "King Alfred and the Cakes."
It can also connect phrases. "She took Ching out on the terrace and left him sitting on the edge." "One day a Chinese laundry man came by and bought Ching."
The word "and" can even connect sentences: "Outside a wise old Chinese owl looked in and the moon shone."
Other popular conjunctions are "but" and "or." "The rubbish man took Ching to his rubbish yard but he had to put him in a separate place." "Ching did not find a home at the tea merchants or hanging in the tree or in the rubbish can."

Other words that can be used as conjunctions are "after" "until" "therefore" or "however." >>

To demonstrate the "joining" function of conjunctions, hold up a piece of paper and rip it in half. Then tape it together. The tape is the "conjunction" and the paper represents words or phrases.

Next have each student choose two sentences from the sequencing activity. Write the words "and" or "but" on pieces of masking tape. The students will connect the two sentences with one of the tape pieces, so a new, longer sentence is made out of the two shorter sentences that will now be joined with a conjunction.

You may wish to have the students write the definition of a conjunction on an index card to add to their other cards for practice at home.

Play "Grammar Tic Tac Toe", "ID Tic Tac Toe", "Kaboom," or "Name That Noun" to review past grammatical concepts, if time.

Choose two or three students to read their finished stories from last week, if time permits.

Homework:
Day 1: Copywork, page 137.
Day 2: Vocabulary, page 138.
Day 3: Read Grammar Lesson, page 139. Conjunctions, page 140.
Day 4: Read the story again. Write the rough draft, using instructions and checklist on page 141 to self-edit.

Lesson 24

Story: "The Travels of Ching" – Robert Bright
Grammar Lesson: Conjunctions

Class-Time: Ask one or two students to share their rough drafts with the class. Later, collect the rough drafts and mark suggestions for changes before handing them back at the end of the day.

Choose a fable from <u>Fables</u> by Arnold Lobel to read together. Discuss: Who are the main characters? What is the main problem/conflict? How is it solved? What is the moral? What can we learn from this story?

Review the definitions of nouns, pronouns, verbs, adjectives, adverbs, prepositions and conjunctions. Review the State-of-Being Verbs Chant and "Yankee Doodle Prepositions."

Do the Silly Sentence activity from Appendix A. Give each student a copy and do the exercise orally together. Students will have fun making silly sentences by combining the different phrases and conjunctions.

Play "Grammar Tic Tac Toe", "ID Tic Tac Toe", "Kaboom," or "Name That Noun" to review past grammatical concepts, if time.

Homework:
Day 1: Spelling Practice, page 142 and Conjunction Practice, page 143.
Day 2: Write the final draft using pages 144-145. Ideas for creative touches are in the student workbook. Students will use provided checklists to self-edit. Additionally, have the parent check these versions today to make sure the basic story stays the same and to correct any spelling or grammatical errors. The final story will be re-copied on Day 4.
Day 3: Parts of Speech chart, page 146 and Grammar Review, page 147.
Day 4: The students will copy over the final versions of their stories. You may wish to ask the parents to bring in two copies to class; one for you to check and return and one for you to save.

Lesson 25

Story: "King Canute on the Seashore" – James Baldwin
Grammar Lesson: Interjections

Class-Time: Introduce "King Canute on the Seashore."
Read "King Canute on the Seashore," pages 148-149, out loud with the students and discuss.
Who are the main characters? *(King Canute, the King's officers)*
What is the problem or conflict? *(the officers praise King Canute and his power too much)*
What is the resolution? *(King Canute tries to command the sea to stop coming in; he fails and demonstrates to his officers that no one is as powerful as God)*
Have the students re-tell the story back to you orally.

Review the definitions of nouns, pronouns, verbs, adjectives, adverbs, prepositions and conjunctions. Practice the State-of-Being Verbs chant and "Yankee Doodle Prepositions."

Introduce the Grammar Lesson using page 152.
The students will learn about interjections.

<< *An **interjection** is a word or phrase that expresses surprise or emotion. Interjections are usually followed by either commas or exclamation points.*
> ***Hey**, what's the king doing?*
> ***Wow!** The king's going to get wet!*
> ***Oh no!** The tide is coming in!*
> ***O king**, you are the greatest.*
Here are some examples of other common interjections: Hooray! Alas. Unreal! Oh! Ah! Hmmm. Whoops!>>

Brainstorm as many interjections as you can and write them on the board.
Play "Jumping Interjections." Stand with the students in a circle. Pass the ball to a student across from you while saying an interjection. That student will pass the ball to another student while saying another interjection. See how long you can go without repeating interjections or getting stuck for one. *Optional:* If a student can't come up with one or repeats one, he must sit down. Play until you have a winner.

You may wish to have the students write the definition of an interjection on an index card to add to their other cards for practice at home.

Play "Grammar Tic Tac Toe", "ID Tic Tac Toe", "Kaboom," or "Name That Noun" to review past grammatical concepts, if time.

Choose two or three students to read their finished stories from last week, if time permits.

Homework:
Day 1: Copywork, page 150.
Day 2: Vocabulary, page 151.
Day 3: Read Grammar Lesson, page 152. Interjections, page 153.
Day 4: Read the story again. Write the rough draft, using instructions and checklist on page 154 to self-edit.

Lesson 26

Story: "King Canute on the Seashore" – James Baldwin
Grammar Lesson: Interjections

Class-Time: Ask one or two students to share their rough drafts with the class. Later, collect the rough drafts and mark suggestions for changes before handing them back at the end of the day.

Read Fantastic! Wow! And Unreal! A Book about Interjections and Conjunctions by Ruth Heller.

Review the definitions of nouns, pronouns, verbs, adjectives, adverbs, prepositions, conjunctions and interjections. Review the State-of-Being Verbs Chant and "Yankee Doodle Prepositions."

Play "Jumping Interjections."

Play "ID Tic Tac Toe", adding the new conjunction and interjection cards from Appendix A.

Homework:
Day 1: Spelling Practice, page 155 and Interjection Practice, page 156.
Day 2: Write the final draft using page 157. Ideas for creative touches are in the student workbook. Students will use provided checklists to self-edit. Additionally, have the parent check these versions today to make sure the basic story stays the same and to correct any spelling or grammatical errors. The final story will be re-copied on Day 4.

Day 3: Parts of Speech chart, page 158 and Grammar Review, page 159.

Day 4: The students will copy over the final versions of their stories. You may wish to ask the parents to bring in two copies to class; one for you to check and return and one for you to save.

Lesson 27

Story: "The Three Goats Named Bruse" – James Baldwin
Grammar Lesson: Review

Class-Time: Introduce "The Three Goats Named Bruse."
Read "The Three Goats Named Bruse," pages 160-161, out loud with the students and discuss.
Who are the main characters? *(the three goats and the Troll)*
What is the problem or conflict? *(the goats want to cross the bridge to get to the better pasture; the Troll will not let them)*
What is the resolution? *(the goats convince the Troll to wait for the biggest goat to eat; the Troll does not realize that the biggest goat is big enough to defend himself)*
Have the students re-tell the story back to you orally.

Use the Storyboard chart from Appendix A to help the students sequence the events. They should draw the major events of the story in each square.

Review the definitions of nouns, pronouns, verbs, adjectives, adverbs, prepositions, conjunctions and interjections. Practice the State-of-Being Verbs chant and "Yankee Doodle Prepositions."

The students have now learned all 8 parts of speech. Technically, every word in the English language can be identified as one of these parts of speech. However, the students are not yet equipped to identify all of them. For example, articles such as "a", "an" or "the" function as adjectives because they are used to modify nouns, but since they do not obviously "decorate" the nouns, the students will have difficulty identifying them as adjectives. This skill will be mastered when they are older.

Write the following sentence on the board:

They eagerly crossed the high bridge over the waterfall.

Circle and label each word as you identify it together.
-Have the students find the nouns (*bridge, waterfall*).
-Have the students find any pronouns (*They*).

-Have the students find the verb (you could ask, "What did they <u>do</u>?" *crossed*).
-Have the students find any adjectives (*the, high, the*). *You may wish to explain briefly that since the word "the" is referring to the nouns "bridge" and "waterfall" it qualifies as an adjective. Don't worry if they don't comprehend this right now. They will eventually, and they are not required to identify anything this hard in their workbooks at this point.*
-Have the students find any adverbs (*eagerly*).
-Have the students find any prepositions (*over*). Sing through "Yankee Doodle Prepositions" if they have trouble.
-Have the students look for conjunctions (*there aren't any*).
-Have the students look for interjections (*there aren't any*).

When you finish, you should have circled and identified every word in the sentence.

Play "Grammar Tic Tac Toe", "ID Tic Tac Toe", "Kaboom," "Jumping Interjections" or "Name That Noun" to review past grammatical concepts, if time.

Choose two or three students to read their finished stories from last week, if time permits.

Homework:
Day 1: Copywork, page 162.
Day 2: Vocabulary, page 163.
Day 3: Grammar Review - Types of Sentences, page 164.
Day 4: Read the story again. Write the rough draft, using instructions and checklist on page 165 to self-edit.

Lesson 28

Story: "The Three Goats Named Bruse" – James Baldwin
Grammar Lesson: Review

Class-Time: Ask one or two students to share their rough drafts with the class. Later, collect the rough drafts and mark suggestions for changes before handing them back at the end of the day.

Choose a fable from Squids Will Be Squids to read together. Discuss: Who are the main characters? What is the main problem/conflict? How is it solved? What is the moral? What can we learn from this story?

Choose a sentence from the fable you read and write it on the board. Practice circling and identifying each word just as in the last lesson.

Play "Grammar Tic Tac Toe", "ID Tic Tac Toe", "Kaboom," "Jumping Interjections" or "Name That Noun" to review past grammatical concepts, if time.

Homework:
Day 1: Spelling Practice, page 166 and Crossword, page 167.
Day 2: Write the final draft using page 168. Ideas for creative touches are in the student workbook. Students will use provided checklists to self-edit. Additionally, have the parent check these versions today to make sure the basic story stays the same and to correct any spelling or grammatical errors. The final story will be re-copied on Day 4.
Day 3: Grammar Review, page 169.
Day 4: The students will copy over the final versions of their stories. You may wish to ask the parents to bring in two copies to class; one for you to check and return and one for you to save.

Lesson 29

Story: "The Story of William Tell" – James Baldwin
Grammar Lesson: Review

Class-Time: Introduce "The Story of William Tell."

Read "The Story of William Tell," pages 170-171, out loud with the students and discuss.
Who are the main characters? *(the tyrant Gessler, William Tell, William Tell's son)*
What is the problem or conflict? *(Tell laughs at Gessler's ridiculous order that he should bow down to his hat; Gessler orders Tell to shoot an apple off of his son's head as punishment)*
What is the resolution? *(Tell shoots the apple without hurting his son; later Tell shoots Gessler and frees his country from tyranny)*
Have the students re-tell the story back to you orally.

Use the Storyboard chart from Appendix A to help the students sequence the events. They should draw the major events of the story in each square.

Review all Parts of Speech Definitions. Practice the State-of-Being Verbs chant and "Yankee Doodle Prepositions."

Play "Grammar Tic Tac Toe", "ID Tic Tac Toe", "Kaboom," "Jumping Interjections" or "Name That Noun" to review past grammatical concepts, if time.

If you are planning on publishing the year's finished stories, have the class design a cover and brainstorm a title for their "book." See more information about this after Lesson 30.

Choose two or three students to read their finished stories from last week, if time permits.

Homework:
Day 1: Copywork, page 172.
Day 2: Vocabulary, page 173.
Day 3: Quotation Review, page 174.
Day 4: Read the story again. Write the rough draft, using instructions and checklist on page 175 to self-edit.

Lesson 30

Story: "The Story of William Tell" – James Baldwin
Grammar Lesson: Review

Class-Time: Ask one or two students to share their rough drafts with the class. Later, collect the rough drafts and mark suggestions for changes before handing them back at the end of the day.

Choose a fable from <u>Fables</u> by Arnold Lobel to read together. Discuss: Who are the main characters? What is the main problem/conflict? How is it solved? What is the moral? What can we learn from this story?

Play "Grammar Tic Tac Toe", "ID Tic Tac Toe", "Kaboom," "Jumping Interjections" or "Name That Noun" to review past grammatical concepts, if time.

Homework:
Day 1: Spelling Practice, page 176.
Day 2: Grammar Review, pages 177-178.
Day 3: Write the final draft using page 179. Ideas for creative touches are in the student workbook. Students will use provided checklists to self-edit. Additionally, have the parent check these versions today to make sure the basic story stays the same and to correct any spelling or grammatical errors. The final story will be re-copied on Day 4.
Day 4: The students will copy over the final versions of their stories. Make sure you get an extra copy of it to put with the others.

****

Don't let the course end without missing an opportunity to "publish" the students' stories! You may choose to publish each student's 15 stories in a book just for them, or you may publish all of the class' stories in one volume and then reproduce it for each student to keep.

In these days of computers, copy machines, and the abundance of office supply and copy stores around, publishing is easy! For a nominal fee a copy store will put a spiral binding on your papers and add a cardboard back cover and a transparent front cover. Why not have the students come up with their own cover design and title for the book? Then reproduce it along with their stories and have a binding put on. The students will have a book that they will cherish their whole lives.

Student Workbook
Answer Key

The Crow and the Pitcher
Copywork

Copy the following sentence from our story. Make sure your sentence has beginning capitals and end punctuation!

Then a thought came to him, and he took a pebble and dropped it into the Pitcher.

Check that the student has copied the passage correctly. Check spelling, capital letters and punctuation.

The Crow and the Pitcher
Aesop

A Crow, half-dead with thirst, came upon a Pitcher which had once been full of water; but when the Crow put its beak into the mouth of the Pitcher he found that only very little water was left in it, and that he could not reach far enough down to get at it. He tried, and he tried, but at last had to give up in despair. Then a thought came to him, and he took a pebble and dropped it into the Pitcher. Then he took another pebble and dropped that into the Pitcher. Then he took another pebble and dropped that into the Pitcher. Then he took another pebble and dropped that into the Pitcher. Then he took another pebble and dropped that into the Pitcher. At last, at last, he saw the water mount up near him, and after casting in a few more pebbles he was able to quench his thirst and save his life.

Moral: Little by little does the trick.

83

The Crow and the Pitcher
Grammar Lesson

Identifying Sentences

1. A sentence starts with a capital letter and ends with a punctuation mark.

   Sentences ALWAYS start with capital letters!
   Sentences will ALWAYS end with either a period, question mark, or exclamation point.

   . ? !

2. A sentence expresses a complete thought.

   Sentences are nice! They will never leave you wondering what they're talking about.

3. A sentence tells us WHO or WHAT, and WHAT THEY DID.

   A sentence will always have a subject, which tells us WHO or WHAT the sentence is about. Also, a sentence will always have a verb, which tells us what the subject did.

The Crow and the Pitcher
Vocabulary

Look up the following words in a dictionary and write down the meanings. Find the words in our story and circle them. Write a short sentence using one of the words.

1. pitcher - **A container with an open top for liquids.**

2. pebble - **A small, round stone.**

3. quench - **To drink until you are no longer thirsty.**

Sentence: _____ **ANSWERS WILL VARY** _____

Remember: your sentence must start with a capital letter and have a punctuation mark at the end!

The Crow and the Pitcher
Sentence Practice

A. Count the number of sentences in our story.

There are __9__ sentences in "The Crow and the Pitcher."

B. Look at the following groups of words and decide if they are sentences or not, using the three sentence requirements. If you answer "no" to any of them, it is not a sentence!!

1. A Crow, half-dead with thirst, came upon a Pitcher which had once been full of water.

	yes	no
Starting capital/end punctuation?	X	
Complete thought?	X	
Subject/Verb?	X	
Is it a sentence?	X	

2. Dropped it into the Pitcher.

	yes	no
Starting capital/end punctuation?	X	
Complete thought?		X
Subject/Verb?		X
Is it a sentence?		X

3. He tried, and he tried, but at last had to give up in despair.

	yes	no
Starting capital/end punctuation?	X	
Complete thought?	X	
Subject/Verb?	X	
Is it a sentence?	X	

4. then he took another pebble and dropped that into the Pitcher

	yes	no
Starting capital/end punctuation?		X
Complete thought?	X	
Subject/Verb?	X	
Is it a sentence?		X

5. At last, at last, he.

	yes	no
Starting capital/end punctuation?	X	
Complete thought?		X
Subject/Verb?		X
Is it a sentence?		X

The Crow and the Pitcher
Spelling Practice

Make a spelling list of up to five words you misspelled and had to correct in your original rough draft. Write each word correctly two times.

1. _____

2. _____ **ANSWERS WILL VARY**

3. _____

4. _____

5. _____

Now choose one of the words and use it in a sentence:

_____

_____

The Crow and the Pitcher
Writing the Rough Draft

Read the story again.

Now it's *your* turn to tell the story. Write your rough draft of "The Crow and the Pitcher," using your own words. Make sure you tell the same story, but as you are choosing which words to use, *you are becoming the author, or writer!*

Edit your writing using the following checklist:

1. Spelling – all the words are spelled correctly. ____

2. Sentences –
   All of your sentences start with capital letters and end with punctuation marks. ____
   They express complete thoughts. ____
   Each one has a subject and a verb. ____

Remember, your goal is to re-write the story of the Crow and the Pitcher in your own words. Creative touches will not be allowed until next week.

The Crow and the Pitcher
The Final Draft

Write your final draft. Now you may add some creative touches, if you like. Here are some suggestions: you may give the Crow a name. You may change what kind of animal he is. As long as the basic story doesn't change, now is the time to make your story individual!

Edit your writing using the following checklist:

1. Spelling – all the words are spelled correctly. ____

2. Sentences –
   All of your sentences start with capital letters and end with punctuation marks. ____
   They express complete thoughts. ____
   Each one has a subject and a verb. ____

Show your finished story to your teacher or parent.

The Crow and the Pitcher
Grammar Lesson – Sentences

Fill in the blanks, using words from the Word Bank:

To be a sentence, a group of words must meet three requirements:

1. It starts with a **capital** letter and ends with a **punctuation** mark.

2. A sentence expresses a complete **thought** it will never leave you **wondering** what it's talking about.

3. A sentence tells us **who** or **what**, and what they **did**.

In other words, it has a **subject** and a **verb**!

Word Bank:

punctuation	verb	wondering	capital	thought
what	did	subject	who	

Answer Key

3. *He took a pebble and.*

Sentence? yes/**no**

He took a pebble and dropped it into the Pitcher.

4. *Then he took another pebble and dropped that into the Pitcher.*

Sentence? **yes**/no

5. *At last, at last, he saw the water mount up near him.*

Sentence? **yes**/no

6. *after casting in a few more pebbles.*

Sentence? yes/**no**

After casting in a few more pebbles he was able to drink.

The Crow and the Pitcher
More Sentence Practice

Decide if the following groups of words are sentences. If not, rewrite them so they ARE sentences.

Example: When the Crow put its beak into the mouth of the Pitcher.

Sentence? yes/**no** *(This is not a complete thought!)*

When the Crow put its beak into the mouth of the Pitcher, he could not reach the water inside.

1. *a Crow came upon a Pitcher*

Sentence? yes/**no**
SENTENCES GIVEN ARE JUST SUGGESTIONS.

A Crow came upon a Pitcher.

2. *He could not reach far enough down to get at it.*

Sentence? **yes**/no

Answer Key   88

The Town Mouse & the Country Mouse
Copywork

Copy the following sentence from our story. Make sure your sentence has beginning capitals and end punctuation!

Beans and bacon, cheese and bread, were all he had to offer, but he offered them freely.

Check that the student has copied the

passage correctly. Check spelling, capital

letters and punctuation.

The Town Mouse and the Country Mouse
Aesop

Now you must know that a Town Mouse once upon a time went on a visit to his cousin in the country. He was rough and ready, this cousin, but he loved his town friend and made him heartily welcome. Beans and bacon, cheese and bread, were all he had to offer, but he offered them freely. The Town Mouse rather turned up his long nose at this country fare, and said, "I cannot understand, Cousin, how you can put up with such poor food as this, but of course you cannot expect anything better in the country; come you with me and I will show you how to live. When you have been in town a week you will wonder how you could ever have stood a country life." No sooner said than done: the two mice set off for the town and arrived at the Town Mouse's residence late at night. "You will want some refreshment after our long journey," said the polite Town Mouse, and took his friend into the grand dining room. There they found the remains of a fine feast, and soon the two mice were eating up jellies and cakes and all that was nice. Suddenly they heard growling and barking. "What is that?" said the Country Mouse. "It is only the dogs of the house," answered the other. "Only!" said the Country Mouse. "I do not like that music at my dinner." Just at that moment the door flew open, in came two huge mastiffs, and the two mice had to scamper down and run off. "Good bye, Cousin," said the Country Mouse. "What! Going so soon?" said the other. "Yes," he replied;

"Better beans and bacon in peace than cakes and ale in fear."

Answer Key

The Town Mouse & the Country Mouse
Grammar Lesson

Kinds of Sentences

There are <u>four</u> different types of sentences.

1. Statement – declares a fact. Statements usually end with periods.

Now you must know that a Town Mouse once upon a time went on a visit to his cousin in the country.

2. Question – asks for information. Questions end with a question mark.

"What is that?"

3. Command – gives an order. Commands usually end with periods, but strong commands could end with exclamation points.

"Come you with me and I will show you how to live."

4. Exclamation – exclaims; shows emotion. Exclamations usually end with exclamation points.

"Only!" or "What!"

The Town Mouse & the Country Mouse
Vocabulary

Look up the following words in a dictionary and write down the meanings. Find the words in our story and circle them. Write a short sentence using one of the words.

1. residence - <u>a place where somebody lives</u>

2. mastiff - <u>an old breed of powerful dog used chiefly</u>

<u>as a watchdog and guard dog</u>

Sentence: _____

ANSWERS WILL VARY

_____

What kind of sentence did you write?

ANSWERS WILL VARY

Statement   Question   Command   Exclamation

The Town Mouse & the Country Mouse
Writing the Rough Draft

Read the story again.

Write your rough draft of "The Town Mouse and the Country Mouse." Tell the same story, but in your *own* words. Make sure your sentences are complete thoughts, and try to show the excitement of the Town Mouse and the calm of the Country Mouse with the words that you choose.

Edit your writing using the following checklist:

1. Spelling – all the words are spelled correctly. ___

2. Sentences –
   All of your sentences start with capital letters and end with punctuation marks. ___
   They express complete thoughts. ___
   Each one has a subject and a verb. ___

Your goal is to re-write the story in your own words. Creative touches will not be allowed until you write the final draft next week.

The Town Mouse & the Country Mouse
Kinds of Sentences

Count the number of sentences in our story.

There are __17__ sentences in "The Town Mouse and the Country Mouse."

Circle the correct classification for each sentence.

1. *He was rough and ready, this cousin, but he loved his town friend and made him heartily welcome.*

   (Statement)   Question   Command   Exclamation

2. *"What!"*

   Statement   Question   Command   (Exclamation)

3. *"Going so soon?"*

   Statement   (Question)   Command   Exclamation

4. *Come with me.*

   Statement   Question   (Command)   Exclamation

5. *The two mice had to scamper down and run off.*

   (Statement)   Question   Command   Exclamation

The Town Mouse & the Country Mouse
Grammar Lesson Review - Kinds of Sentences

Fill in the blanks using words from the Word Bank.

There are __4__ different kinds of sentences.

1. Statement: __declares__ a __fact__ .

2. Question: __asks__ for information.

3. Command: __gives__ an __order__ .

4. Exclamation: exclaims; __shows__ emotion.

Which kind of sentence ends with a question mark? __question__

Which kind of sentence probably ends with a period? __statement__

Which kind of sentence usually ends with an exclamation point?

__exclamation__

Which kind of sentence could have a period or an exclamation

point? __command__

Word Bank:
shows   four   exclamation   order   asks   fact   question   command   declares   gives   statement

---

The Town Mouse & the Country Mouse
Spelling Practice

Make a spelling list of up to five words you misspelled and had to correct in your original rough draft. Write each word correctly two times.

1. _____

ANSWERS WILL VARY

2. _____

3. _____

4. _____

5. _____

Now choose one of the words and use it in a sentence:

_____

The Town Mouse & the Country Mouse
Four Kinds of Sentences

Change the following sentences as indicated.

Example: *Now you must know that a Town Mouse went on a visit to his cousin.*

Change to a question: <u>*Did the Town Mouse visit his cousin?*</u>

1. *He made him heartily welcome.*

Change to a command: <u>**Make him heartily welcome.**</u>

2. *The two mice set off for the town.*

Change to a question: <u>**Did the two mice set off for town?**</u>

3. *"What is that?" said the Country Mouse.*

Change to a statement: <u>**The Country Mouse asked what that was.**</u>

4. *Suddenly they heard growling and barking.*

Change to an exclamation: <u>**Oh no!** or **Aaah!**</u>

The Town Mouse & the Country Mouse
The Final Draft

Write your final draft. Now you may add some creative touches, if you like. Some suggestions: you may give the mice names. You may change what kind of animals they are. As long as the basic story doesn't change, now is the time to make <u>your</u> story individual!

Edit your writing using the following checklist:

1. Spelling – all the words are spelled correctly. ___

2. Sentences –
   All of your sentences start with capital letters and end with punctuation marks. ___
   They express complete thoughts. ___
   Each one has a subject and a verb. ___

Show your finished story to your teacher or parent.

93   Answer Key

Androcles
Copywork

Copy the following sentence from our story. Make sure your sentence has correct capitals!

As he came near, the Lion put out his paw, which was all swollen and bleeding, and Androcles found that a huge thorn had got into it, and was causing all the pain.

Check that the student has copied the

passage correctly. Check spelling, capital

letters and punctuation.

Androcles
Aesop

A slave named Androcles once escaped from his master and fled to the forest. As he was wandering about there he came upon a Lion lying down moaning and groaning. At first he turned to flee, but finding that the Lion did not pursue him, he turned back and went up to him. As he came near, the Lion put out his paw, which was all swollen and bleeding, and Androcles found that a huge thorn had gotten into it, and was causing all the pain. He pulled out the thorn and bound up the paw of the Lion, who was soon able to rise and lick the hand of Androcles like a dog. Then the Lion took Androcles to his cave, and every day used to bring him meat from which to live. But shortly afterwards both Androcles and the Lion were captured, and the slave was sentenced to be thrown to the Lion, after the latter had been kept without food for several days. The Emperor and all his Court came to see the spectacle, and Androcles was led out into the middle of the arena. Soon the lion was let loose from his den and rushed bounding and roaring towards his victim. But as soon as he came near to Androcles he recognized his friend, and fawned upon him, and licked his hands like a friendly dog. The Emperor, surprised at this, summoned Androcles to him, who told him the whole story. Whereupon the slave was pardoned and freed, and the Lion let loose to his native forest.

Gratitude is the sign of noble souls.

Androcles
Grammar Lesson
4 Rules of Capitalization

1. **Sentences** start with a capital letter. We've already learned about this rule!

2. **Titles** begin with capital letters. Titles like *Mr., Mrs., Miss,* or *Dr.* always start with capital letters. The important words in book, movie, story or song titles always start with capital letters. For example, our stories, *"Androcles"* or *"The Town Mouse and the Country Mouse."*

3. **Proper Names** begin with capital letters. Specific names of people, places or things always start with capital letters, because we want to recognize that they are special and unique. For example, the city of *Boston* is special and unique, so we capitalize the "B". *Kristen, Timothy* and *Melissa* are all special and unique people, so we begin their names with capital letters. And the *Frisbee* is a very special and unique toy, so its name starts with a capital letter too!

4. The word **"I"** is always capitalized. Are you special and unique? Of course you are! Then always capitalize the word "I"!

Androcles
Vocabulary

Look up the following words in a dictionary and write down the meanings. Find the words in our story and circle them. Write a short sentence using one of the words.

1. pursue -   to follow or chase someone in order to

   catch him or her

2. spectacle - a remarkable and dramatic sight

3. summon - to call or request someone to come

   ANSWERS WILL VARY

Sentence: _____

What kind of sentence did you write?

Statement   Question   Command   Exclamation

3. then the lion took androcles to his cave.

4. but shortly afterwards both androcles and the lion

were captured.

5. whereupon the slave was pardoned and freed, and the

lion let loose to his native forest.

6. i love aesop's stories!

7. my favorite story is "the town mouse and the country

mouse."

8. aesop lived in greece a long time ago.

Androcles

Capitalization Practice

1. **Sentences** start with a capital letter.
2. **Titles** begin with capital letters.
3. **Proper Names** begin with capital letters.
4. The word "**I**" is always capitalized.

Circle the words that need to be capitalized, and tell which rule says why.

Example: i think our story "androcles" is exciting.
Rules 1 and 4 tell us why "i" should be capitalized: it is the beginning of the sentence, AND it is the word "I". Rules 2 and 3 tell us why "androcles" should be capitalized: it is the name of our story AND it is the name of a unique person.

* Remember that in our story, the Lion has his name capitalized because we are not talking about just any lion, we are talking about one specific Lion.

1. a slave named androcles once escaped from his master

and fled to the forest.

2. as he came near, the lion put out his paw, and

androcles found that a huge thorn had got into it.

Androcles
Spelling Practice

Make a spelling list of up to five words you misspelled and had to correct in your original rough draft. Write each word correctly two times.

1. _____

ANSWERS WILL VARY

2. _____

3. _____

4. _____

5. _____

Now choose one of the words and use it in a sentence:

_____

Androcles
Writing the Rough Draft

Read the story again. Write your rough draft of "Androcles." Tell the same story, but in your *own* words. Choose words that might show the pain of the lion, the deep friendship that grows between Androcles and the lion, and perhaps the surprise of the Emperor. When you are finished, read each sentence out loud to make sure it is a complete thought.

Edit your writing using the following checklist:

1. Spelling – all the words are spelled correctly. ____

2. Sentences –
   All of your sentences end with punctuation marks. ____
   They express complete thoughts. ____
   Each one has a subject and a verb. ____

3. Capitalization –
   All the important words in the title begin with capital letters. ____
   Every sentence begins with a capital letter. ____
   The word "I" is capitalized, if used. ____
   All proper names start with capital letters. ____

Your goal is to re-write the story in your own words. Stick to the basic story for this week.

Androcles
The Final Draft

Write your final draft. Now you may add some creative touches, if you like. Some suggestions: you may give the lion a name. You may change the setting. You may change what was causing the Lion pain in the beginning. You may even change the Lion to a different kind of animal, but be careful to do your research. The animal should be one that is not normally kind to people. In fact, it should be one that is known for *eating* people! As long as the basic story doesn't change, now is the time to make your story individual.

Edit your writing using the following checklist:

1. Spelling – all the words are spelled correctly. ___

2. Sentences –
   All of your sentences end with punctuation marks. ___
   They express complete thoughts. ___
   Each one has a subject and a verb. ___

3. Capitalization –
   All the important words in the title begin with
   capital letters. ___
   Every sentence begins with a capital letter. ___
   The word "I" is capitalized, if used. ___
   All proper names start with capital letters. ___

Show your finished story to your teacher or parent.

Androcles
Capitalization

In the reading passage below, circle all the letters which should be capitalized.

(A)ndrocles (c)ontinued

(B)ut as soon as he came near to (A)ndrocles he recognized

his friend, and fawned upon him, and licked his hands like

a friendly dog. (t)he (e)mperor surprised at this, summoned

(A)ndrocles to him, who told him the whole story.

(w)hereupon the slave was pardoned and freed, and the lion

let loose to his native forest.

Androcles
Capitalization Review

1. Write a sentence about our story's title, including the title and proper capitalization.

_____

_____

2. Write a sentence about a hero of our story, using proper capitalization of his name.

ANSWERS WILL VARY

_____

CHECK FOR PROPER CAPITALIZATION

_____

3. Write a sentence about how you liked "Androcles".

_____

_____

What kind of sentence did you write?

Statement   Question   *Command*   Exclamation

Julius Caesar
James Baldwin

Nearly two thousand years ago there lived in Rome a man whose name was Julius Caesar. He was the greatest of all the Romans. Why was he so great?

He was a brave warrior, and had conquered many countries for Rome. He was wise in planning and in doing. He knew how to make men both love and fear him. At last he made himself the ruler of Rome. Some said that he wished to become its king. But the Romans at that time did not believe in kings.

Once when Caesar was passing through a little country village, all the men, women, and children of the place came out to see him. There were not more than fifty of them, all together, and they were led by their mayor, who told each one what to do. These simple people stood by the roadside and watched Caesar pass. The mayor looked very proud and happy, for was he not the ruler of this village? He felt that he was almost as great a man as Caesar himself.

Some of the fine officers who were with Caesar laughed. They said, "See how that fellow struts at the head of his little flock!"

"Laugh as you will," said Caesar, "he has reason to be proud. I would rather be the head man of a village than the second man in Rome!"

At another time, Caesar was crossing a narrow sea in a boat. Before he was halfway to the farther shore, a storm overtook him. The wind blew hard; the waves clashed high; the lightning flashed;

Julius Caesar
Copywork

Copy the following passage from our story. Make sure you copy the correct capital letters and punctuation.

Nearly two thousand years ago there lived in Rome a man whose name was Julius Caesar. He was the greatest of all the Romans.

Check that the student has copied the

passage correctly. Check spelling, capital

letters and punctuation.

---

the thunder rolled. It seemed every minute as though the boat would sink. The captain was in great fright. He had crossed the sea many times, but never in such a storm as this. He trembled with fear; he could not guide the boat; he fell down upon his knees; he moaned, "All is lost! All is lost!"

But Caesar was not afraid. He bade the man get up and take his oars again. "Why should you be afraid?" he said. "The boat will not be lost; for you have Caesar on board."

Julius Caesar
Grammar Lesson
Punctuation Traffic Signals

For this grammar lesson, let's think of punctuation as the traffic signals in our writing. The punctuation marks tell us when to slow down and when to stop, and help to keep our words from bumping into each other.

The Red Lights: These are the easy ones, and we've already learned them! Think of the period, the exclamation point, and the question mark as "red lights." When you see them, the sentence stops! Don't start moving again until you see the "green light" of the next sentence's beginning capital letter.

The Yield Signs: Commas act like yield signs; they tell you to slow down before proceeding. Take a breath, look around, and then continue on with your journey of reading the sentence.

The Stop Signs: Semi-colons act like stop signs. They tell the reader to slow down and stop before continuing on again.

Julius Caesar
Vocabulary

Look up the following words in a dictionary and write down the meanings. Find the words in our story and circle them. Write a short sentence using one of the words.

1. warrior - A soldier, or someone who is experienced in

fighting battles.

2. mayor - The leader of a town or city government.

3. strut - To walk with a swagger or in an arrogant

manner.

Sentence: _____ **ANSWERS WILL VARY**

101

Answer Key

Student Page 40 – Lesson 7

Julius Caesar
Writing the Rough Draft

Read the story again. Write your rough draft of "Julius Caesar." Tell the same story, but in your *own* words. Choose words that might show the bravery and wisdom of Caesar as well as the pride and joy of the village mayor. Use words that will show the excitement of the storm at sea. When you are finished, read each sentence out loud to make sure it is a complete thought.

Edit your writing using the following checklist:

1. Spelling – all the words are spelled correctly. ___
2. Sentences – ___
   Each sentence expresses a complete thought. ___
   Each one has a subject and a verb. ___
3. Capitalization –
   All the important words in the title begin with
   capital letters. ___
   Every sentence begins with a capital letter. ___
   The word "I" is capitalized, if used. ___
   All proper names start with capital letters. ___
4. Punctuation –
   All of your sentences end with periods or
   exclamation marks.
   Any questions end with question marks. ___

Your goal is to re-write the story in your own words. Stick to the basic story for this week.

Student Page 39 – Lesson 7

Julius Caesar
Punctuation Practice

1. **End punctuations** (! . and ?) are the red lights. Stop! Beginning Capital Letters are the green lights.
2. **Commas** (,) are the yield signs. Slow down!
3. **Semi-colons** (;) are the stop signs. Slow down and stop, then go on.

In each sentence, put a red box around the periods or exclamation points for stop. Circle the commas with yellow for slow down. Circle the semi-colons with red for stop, and then go on. Circle the beginning capital letters of each sentence in green for go. Practice reading the sentences out loud while obeying the "traffic signals."

1. He was a brave warrior, and had conquered many countries for Rome.

2. Once when Caesar was passing through a little country village, all the men, women, and children of the place came out to see him.

3. The wind blew hard; the waves clashed high; the lightning flashed; the thunder rolled.

4. He trembled with fear; he could not guide the boat; he fell down upon his knees; he moaned, "All is lost! All is lost!"

Julius Caesar
Punctuation Review

1. Write a sentence about Julius Caesar that ends in a period.

_____

_____

2. Write a sentence about Julius Caesar that ends in a question mark.

_____

ANSWERS WILL VARY

_____

3. Write a sentence about Julius Caesar that ends in an exclamation point.

_____

_____

Julius Caesar
Spelling Practice

Make a spelling list of up to five words you misspelled and had to correct in your original rough draft. Write each word correctly two times.

1. _____   _____

ANSWERS WILL VARY

2. _____   _____

3. _____   _____

4. _____   _____

5. _____   _____

Now choose one of the words and use it in a sentence:

_____

Julius Caesar

Will the Real Punctuation Please Stand Up?

Imposters lurk nearby! Some wayward punctuation marks are trying to sneak in where they don't belong. Read the sentences below, using the "traffic signals" for pausing and stopping, and circle the letter of the sentence that has the correct punctuation.

1.
  A. Nearly two, thousand years ago there! lived in Rome a man whose name was Julius Caesar?

  B. Nearly! two thousand years, ago there lived in Rome a man whose name was, Julius Caesar.

  C. Nearly two thousand years ago there lived in Rome a man whose name was Julius Caesar. *(circled)*

2.
  A. Why was he so great? *(circled)*

  B. Why, was he so great.

  C. Why was he so great!

3.
  A. He was a brave warrior and, had conquered many countries for Rome.

  B. He, was a brave warrior and had conquered, many countries for Rome.

  C. He was a brave warrior, and had conquered many countries for Rome. *(circled)*

4.
  A. At another time Caesar, was crossing a narrow sea in a boat!

  B. At another time, Caesar was crossing a narrow sea in a boat. *(circled)*

  C. At, another time, Caesar was, crossing a narrow sea in a boat.

Julius Caesar
The Final Draft

Write your final draft. Now you may add some creative touches. However, we have to be careful with this story, since it is about a real person. Do not change any main characters or basic events or settings. You may change little things that will not affect the story. For example, you may want to describe some of the village people who watched Caesar pass by in the third paragraph. Why were they excited? What kinds of things did they say to one another or to Caesar as he passed? You may want to name the officer who speaks to Caesar in the fourth paragraph. Or you may want to tell us why you think Caesar needed to cross the sea in the last two paragraphs.

Edit your writing using the following checklist:

1. Spelling – all the words are spelled correctly. _____
2. Sentences – _____

  Each sentence expresses a complete thought. _____
  Each one has a subject and a verb. _____

3. Capitalization –

  All the important words in the title begin with capital letters. _____
  Every sentence begins with a capital letter. _____
  The word "I" is capitalized, if used. _____
  All proper names start with capital letters. _____

4. Punctuation –

  All of your sentences end with periods or exclamation marks. _____
  Any questions end with question marks. _____

Show your finished story to your teacher or parent.

5. A. It seemed every minute as; though the boat would sink?
    B. It seemed every minute as though the boat would sink.
    C. It! seemed, every minute as though the boat would sink!

6. A. He trembled with fear; he could not guide the boat: he fell down upon his knees; he moaned, "All is lost! All is lost!"
    B. He trembled with fear! he could not guide the boat he fell down upon his knees he moaned: "All is lost? All is lost?"
    C. He trembled, with fear he could, not guide the boat he, fell down upon his, knees he moaned "All is lost, all is lost."

7. A. But Caesar was not afraid.
    B. But Caesar, was not afraid!
    C. But Caesar was not afraid?

8. A. The boat will not be lost! for you have Caesar, on board.
    B. The boat will not be lost; for you have Caesar on board.
    C. The boat will not be lost; for you have Caesar on board?

The Princess and the Pea
Andersen

Once upon a time there was a prince who wanted to marry a princess; but she would have to be a real princess. He traveled all over the world to find one, but nowhere could he get what he wanted. There were princesses enough, but it was difficult to find out whether they were real ones. There was always something about them that was not as it should be. So he came home again and was sad, for he would have liked very much to have a real princess.

One evening a terrible storm came on; there was thunder and lightning, and the rain poured down in torrents. Suddenly a knocking was heard at the city gate, and the old king went to open it.

It was a princess standing out there in front of the gate. But, good gracious! What a sight the rain and the wind had made her look. The water ran down from her hair and clothes; it ran down into the toes of her shoes and out again at the heels. And yet she said that she was a real princess.

"Well, we'll soon find that out," thought the old queen. But she said nothing, went into the bedroom, took all the bedding off the bedstead, and laid a pea on the bottom; then she took twenty mattresses and laid them on the pea, and then twenty eider-down beds on top of the mattresses.

On this the princess had to lie all night. In the morning she was asked how she had slept.

105

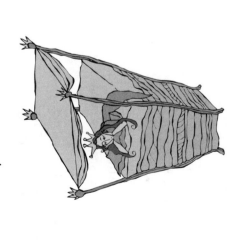

The Princess and the Pea
Copywork

Copy the following sentences from our story. Make sure your sentences have correct capitals and punctuation.

Now they knew that she was a real princess because she had felt the pea right through the twenty mattresses and the twenty eider-down beds. Nobody but a real princess could be as sensitive as that.

Check that the student has copied the passage correctly. Check spelling, capital letters and punctuation.

"Oh, very badly!" said she. "I have scarcely closed my eyes all night. Heaven only knows what was in the bed, but I was lying on something hard, so that I am black and blue all over my body. It's horrible!"

Now they knew that she was a real princess because she had felt the pea right through the twenty mattresses and the twenty eiderdown beds.

Nobody but a real princess could be as sensitive as that.

So the prince took her for his wife, for now he knew that he had a real princess; and the pea was put in the museum, where it may still be seen, if no one has stolen it.

There, that is a true story.

The Princess and the Pea
Grammar Lesson
Simple Quotes

When we talk about quotes in a story, we are talking about words that people are saying.

Direct Quotes are words that the character is actually saying, and are always surrounded by quotation marks .

Example: "Ouch!" cried the princess.

Indirect Quotes are words that the storyteller tells us were said by the characters. They do not have quotation marks .

Example: The princess cried out in pain. or The princess said that she did not sleep well the night before.

Indirect quotes are easy to punctuate; use the same rules we learned for regular sentences. Begin with a capital letter, use commas if you want the reader to pause, semi-colons if you want the reader to stop and then continue on, and always end with a period, exclamation point or question mark.

Direct quotes can be more difficult to punctuate.

-The words actually said by a character must be surrounded by quotation marks .

"I don't think this bed is very comfortable."

-The words inside the quotation marks will always start with a beginning capital letter, just like a sentence.

The Princess and the Pea
Vocabulary

Look up the following words in a dictionary and write down the meanings. Find the words in our story and circle them. Write a short sentence using one of the words.

1. torrent - <u>a swift, violent stream, especially of</u>

<u>water.</u>

2. eiderdown - *(If you cannot find this, look up down and write down the meaning of the noun, NOT the preposition; it will be the same)* <u>the soft, fine down of the eider duck, used as a stuffing for</u>

<u>quilts or pillows.</u>

Sentence: _____ <u>ANSWERS WILL VARY</u>

The Princess and the Pea

Quotations

There are three direct quotes in our story. Find them and underline them in red. *Check that this is done on the story page. Direct quotes are: "Well, we'll soon find out about that," "Oh, very badly!" and "I have scarcely closed my eyes all night...."*

Who says the first quote?

the prince   (the queen)   the princess

Who says the second quote?

the prince   the queen   (the princess)

Who says the third quote?

the prince   the queen   (the princess)

Two of the following quotes are punctuated correctly. Underline them in red.

"Well, we'll soon find that out." thought the old queen.

"Oh, very badly!" said she.

"We will put the pea in a museum," said the prince.

The princess said. "I was lying on something hard."

-If the narrator introduces the quote (*She said, "Ouch!"*), there will be a comma before the quotation marks, because you want the reader to pause before reading the quote, and end punctuation at the end inside the quotation marks to show that the sentence is finished.

He asked, "Why didn't you sleep well?"

-If the narrator finishes the quote instead (*"Ouch," she said.*) AND the quote from the character was a sentence that should end in a period, then a comma is put at the end of the quote, inside the quotation marks, so that there will be a pause before finishing the sentence, and the end punctuation will be put at the end, after the narrator concludes the sentence.

"I need more mattresses," said the queen.

-If the character says in a direct quote something that would end with an exclamation point or a question mark, these are left in the quote, and the sentence will still end with an end punctuation mark after the narrator finishes it.

"Why didn't you sleep well?" he asked.
"Goodness gracious!" she cried.

The Princess and the Pea
Spelling Practice

Make a spelling list of up to five words you misspelled and had to correct in your original rough draft. Write each word correctly two times.

1. _____

2. _____

ANSWERS WILL VARY

3. _____

4. _____

5. _____

Now choose one of the words and use it in a sentence:

_____

_____

The Princess and the Pea
Writing the Rough Draft

Read the story again. Write your rough draft of "The Princess and the Pea." Tell the same story, but in your *own* words. Be sure to describe how difficult it had been for the prince to find a real princess in his travels. Find words to describe how the princess looked when she arrived at the castle gate. Be sure the princess complains a lot about how much the pea hurt her, even through all those soft mattresses! When you are finished, read each sentence out loud to make sure it is a complete thought.

Edit your writing using the following checklist:

1. Spelling – all the words are spelled correctly. _____
2. Sentences –
   Each sentence expresses a complete thought. _____
   Each one has a subject and a verb. _____
3. Capitalization –
   All the important words in the title begin with capital letters. _____
   Every sentence begins with a capital letter. _____
   The word "I" is capitalized, if used. _____
   All proper names start with capital letters. _____
4. Punctuation –
   All of your sentences end with periods or exclamation marks. _____
   Any questions end with question marks. _____
5. Quotes –
   You have included at least one direct quote. _____
   You used quotation marks around the words spoken. _____

Answer Key

The Princess and the Pea
Final Draft

Write your final draft. Now you may add some creative touches. Let's keep the main characters as a prince and a princess, but can you think of some different things to add to the story? When the prince first went out to find a princess, why couldn't he tell if any of them were real princesses? How about the princess herself – when she knocks on the door in the middle of the storm, does she have an explanation for what she was doing out on such a terrible night? See what else you can come up with.

Edit your writing using the following checklist:

1. Spelling – all the words are spelled correctly. |
2. Sentences – |
   Each sentence expresses a complete thought. |
   Each one has a subject and a verb. |
3. Capitalization –
   All the important words in the title begin with capital letters. |
   Every sentence begins with a capital letter. |
   The word "I" is capitalized, if used. |
   All proper names start with capital letters. |
4. Punctuation –
   All of your sentences end with periods or exclamation marks. |
   Any questions end with question marks. |
5. Quotes –
   You have included at least one direct quote. |
   You used quotation marks around the words spoken. |

Show your finished story to your teacher or parent.

The Princess and the Pea
Practice with Simple Quotes

Label each quote as <u>direct</u> (D) or <u>indirect</u> (I). If it is a direct quote, find and circle the quotation marks in purple. Circle all end punctuation (! . or ?) in red.

1. __I__ The prince said that he could not find a real princess on his travels.

2. __D__ The old king asked, "Do you hear that knocking at the city gate?"

3. __D__ The princess apologized, "I have been caught in the storm without my umbrella!"

4. __D__ The king later reported, "What a sight she was!"

5. __I__ And yet she said that she was a real princess.

6. __D__ "Well, we'll soon find that out," thought the old queen.

4. *"Oh, very badly!" said she.*

<u>She said that she had slept very badly.</u>

5. *"Will you marry me?" asked the prince.*

<u>The prince asked her to marry him.</u>

The Princess and the Pea
Quotations

Change the following indirect quotes into direct quotes.
Example: The old king went to open the door.
   <u>*"I am going to open the door," said the old king.*</u>

1. *Once upon a time there was a prince who wanted to marry a princess; but she would have to be a real princess.*

<u>**"I want to marry a princess, but she has to be a real princess," said the prince.**</u>

2. *So he came home again and was sad, for he would have liked very much to have a real princess.*

<u>**The prince said, "I am sad, because I would very much like to have a real princess."**</u>

Change the following direct quotes into indirect quotes.
Example: "I am a real princess," said she.
   <u>*She said that she was a real princess.*</u>

3. *"How did you sleep, princess?" asked the old queen.*

<u>**The old queen asked the princess how she slept.**</u>

THE ELVES AND THE SHOEMAKER

by Horace E. Scudder

There was once a shoemaker who worked very hard and was honest. Still, he could not earn enough to live on. At last, all he had in the world was gone except just leather enough to make one pair of shoes. He cut these out at night, and meant to rise early the next morning to make them up.

His heart was light in spite of his troubles, for his conscience was clear. So he went quietly to bed, left all his cares to God, and fell asleep. In the morning he said his prayers, and sat down to work, when, to his great wonder, there stood the shoes, already made, upon the table.

The good man knew not what to say or think. He looked at the work. There was not one false stitch in the whole job. All was neat and true.

That same day a customer came in, and the shoes pleased him so well that he readily paid a price higher than usual for them. The shoemaker took the money and bought leather enough to make two pairs more. He cut out the work in the evening, and went to bed early. He wished to be up with the sun and get to work.

He was saved all trouble, for when he got up in the morning, the work was done. Pretty soon buyers came in, who paid him well for his goods. So he bought leather enough for four pairs more.

He cut out the work again overnight, and found it finished in the morning as before. So it went on for some time. What was got ready at night was always done by daybreak, and the good man soon was well-to-do.

One evening, at Christmas-time, he and his wife sat over the fire, chatting, and he said: "I should like to sit up and watch to-night, that we may see who it is that comes and does my work for me." So they left the light burning, and hid themselves behind a curtain to see what would happen.

The Princess and the Pea
Grammar Review

Identify the following sentences as statements (S), questions (Q), exclamations (E), or commands (C).

1. **S** Then she took twenty mattresses and laid them on the pea, and then twenty eider-down beds on top of the mattresses.

2. **S** In the morning she was asked how she slept.

3. **E** "It's horrible!"

4. **Q** Why did she feel the pea right through twenty mattresses and twenty eider-down beds?

5. **S** Nobody but a real princess could be as sensitive as that.

6. **C** Put that pea in the museum.

7. **S** There, that is a true story.

Answer Key   112

The Elves and the Shoemaker
Copywork

Copy the following sentences from our story. Make sure your sentences have correct capitals and punctuation.

At midnight the Elves came in and were going to sit down at their work as usual. But when they saw the clothes lying there for them, they laughed and were in high glee.

Check that the student has copied the passage correctly. Check spelling, capital letters and punctuation.

As soon as it was midnight, there came two little Elves. They sat upon the shoemaker's bench, took up all the work that was cut out, and began to ply their little fingers. They stitched and rapped and tapped at such a rate that the shoemaker was amazed, and could not take his eyes off them for a moment.

On they went till the job was done, and the shoes stood, ready for use, upon the table. This was long before daybreak. Then they ran away as quick as lightning.

The next day the wife said to the shoemaker: "These little Elves have made us rich, and we ought to be thankful to them, and do them some good in return. I am vexed to see them run about as they do. They have nothing upon their backs to keep off the cold. I'll tell you what we must do. I will make each of them a shirt, and a coat and waistcoat, and a pair of pantaloons into the bargain. Do you make each of them a little pair of shoes."

The good shoemaker liked the thought very well. One evening he and his wife had the clothes ready, and laid them on the table instead of the work they used to cut out. Then they went and hid behind the curtain to watch what the little Elves would do.

At midnight the Elves came in and were going to sit down at their work as usual. But when they saw the clothes lying there for them, they laughed and were in high glee. They dressed themselves in the twinkling of an eye, and danced and capered and sprang about as merry as could be, till at last they danced out of the door and over the green.

The shoemaker saw them no more, but everything went well with him as long as he lived.

Nouns are circled per instructions in the Teacher's Guide Lesson Plans, Lesson 12. Note that some of these nouns are difficult! The student may or may not find all of them. Also note that the word "work" is used both as a noun AND as a verb in this story: be careful to point out the difference if necessary.

The Elves and the Shoemaker
Grammar Lesson
Nouns

<u>A noun</u> is the name of a person, place, thing, or idea.

Examples:

People – elves, shoemaker, customer, wife

Places – shop, village, workroom, street

Things – shoe, leather, stitch, curtain, bench

Ideas – honesty, love, hope, wonder, troubles

Most nouns are called *Common Nouns.* Nouns that name specific people or places are called *Proper Nouns.* Proper Nouns always start with capital letters.
Example: Sally, John, Mr. Jones, Seattle, Boston

The Elves and the Shoemaker
Vocabulary

Look up the following words in a dictionary and write down the meanings. Find the words in our story and circle them. Write a short sentence using one of the words.

1. ply – <u>   to keep busy or work; to work at a trade   </u>

_____

2. vexed – <u>   (vex) to annoy or irritate somebody   </u>

_____

3. capered – <u>   to skip about in a playful manner   </u>

_____

_____

Sentence: _____

_____

The Elves and the Shoemaker
Writing the Rough Draft

Read the story again. Write your rough draft of "The Elves and the Shoemaker." This is the longest story we have had so far! Remember to describe the honest, hardworking shoemaker and how he had nothing left in the world but leather to make one last pair of shoes. How did he feel the next morning when he discovered the wonderfully made pair of shoes waiting for him? What did he and his wife think of the two little Elves when they saw them from behind the curtain? Describe how thrilled the Elves were when they discovered their new clothes. When you are finished, read each sentence out loud to make sure it is a complete thought.

Edit your writing using the following checklist:

1. Spelling – all the words are spelled correctly.
2. Sentences –
   Each sentence expresses a complete thought.
   Each one has a subject and a verb.
3. Capitalization –
   All the important words in the title begin with capital letters.
   Every sentence begins with a capital letter.
   The word "I" is capitalized, if used.
   All proper names start with capital letters.
4. Punctuation –
   All of your sentences end with periods or exclamation marks.
   Any questions end with question marks.
5. Quotes –
   You have included at least one direct quote.
   You used quotation marks around the words spoken.

The Elves and the Shoemaker
Nouns

A noun is the name of a person, place, thing, or idea.

Find two nouns in our story that name *people:*

1.   **shoemaker**   2.   **customer**

could also be elves, wife, man, buyers

Give a noun that names a *place* in our story:

1.   **workshop**

There are actually no nouns in the story that clearly name a place, but a workshop is implied, as is a village, a cottage, etc.

Find three nouns that name *things:*

1.   **shoes**   2.   **bed**   3.   **table**

could also be stitch, bench, fire, work, light, curtain

Find one noun that names an *idea:*

1.   **conscience, wonder**

The Elves and the Shoemaker
Noun Practice

Circle all of the nouns in the following passage from our story:

That same day a customer came in, and the shoes pleased him so well that he readily paid a price higher than usual for them. The shoemaker took the money and bought leather enough to make two pairs more. He cut out the work in the evening and went to bed early. He wished to be up with the sun and get to work.

Make up a name for the customer: _____
CHECK FOR CORRECT CAPITALIZATION
Make up a name for the shoemaker: _____

Did you use correct capitalization? _____

The Elves and the Shoemaker
Spelling Practice

Make a spelling list of up to five words you misspelled and had to correct in your original rough draft. Write each word correctly two times.

1. _____

2. _____

ANSWERS WILL VARY

3. _____

4. _____

5. _____

Now choose one of the words and use it in a sentence:

_____

_____

The Eight Parts of Speech

Fill in the top right box with examples of different types of nouns. Memorize the definition of a noun.

Definitions	Examples
A Noun is a name for a person, place, thing or idea.	Check that the student has listed several nouns here.

The Elves and the Shoemaker
Final Draft

Write your final draft. Now you may add some creative touches. Let's try to keep the basic story and events. Will you keep the shoemaker or change his character to another type of tradesman, like a dressmaker or blacksmith? How about the elves...do they have names? And what makes them decide to help out? See what else you can come up with.

Edit your writing using the following checklist:

1. Spelling – all the words are spelled correctly. |
2. Sentences –
   Each sentence expresses a complete thought. |
   Each one has a subject and a verb. |
3. Capitalization –
   All the important words in the title begin with
   capital letters. |
   Every sentence begins with a capital letter. |
   The word "I" is capitalized, if used. |
   All proper names start with capital letters. |
4. Punctuation –
   All of your sentences end with periods or
   exclamation marks. |
   Any questions end with question marks. |
5. Quotes –
   You have included at least one direct quote. |
   You used quotation marks around the words spoken. |

Show your finished story to your teacher or parent.

Answer Key

4. Write an exclamation that the elves might have said when they saw their new clothes:

"Wow!"   "Terrific!"

5. Rewrite, inserting proper names for the shoemaker and his wife AND capitalizing in the right places: *the shoemaker and his wife had the clothes ready, and laid them on the table.*

George and Mary had the clothes ready, and laid them on the table.

The Elves and the Shoemaker
Grammar Review

Rewrite the following sentences as directed.

Example- Rewrite as a question: There once was a shoemaker who worked very hard. <u>*Was there once a shoemaker who worked very hard? or Did the shoemaker work very hard?*</u>

1. Rewrite as a command: *He meant to rise early the next morning to make them up.*

<u>Rise early the next morning and make them up.</u>

2. Rewrite as a question: *There was not one false stitch in the whole job.*

<u>Were there any false stitches in the whole job?</u>

3. Rewrite as a direct quote: *The good shoemaker liked the thought very well.*

<u>"I like that thought very well," said the good shoemaker.</u>

The Cat, the Monkey and the Chestnuts
Copywork

Copy the following sentences from our story. Make sure your sentences have correct capitals and punctuation.

A Cat and a Monkey were sitting one day by the hearth, watching some chestnuts which their master had laid down to roast. The chestnuts had begun to burst with the heat.

_____

Check that the student has copied the passage

correctly. Check spelling, capital letters

and punctuation.

_____

The Cat, the Monkey and the Chestnuts

by Horace E. Scudder

A Cat and a Monkey were sitting one day by the hearth, watching some chestnuts which their master had laid down to roast. The chestnuts had begun to burst with the heat, and the Monkey said to the Cat:

"It is plain that your paws were made to pull out those chestnuts. Your paws are, indeed, exactly like our master's hands."

The Cat was greatly flattered by this speech, and reached forward for the tempting chestnuts. Scarcely had she touched the hot ashes than she drew back with a cry, for she had burned her paw. She tried again, and made out to get one chestnut. Then she pulled another, and a third, though each time she singed the hair on her paws. When she could pull no more, she turned, and found the Monkey had taken this time to crack the chestnuts and eat them.

119

Answer Key

The Cat, the Monkey and the Chestnuts
Grammar Lesson
Pronouns

A **pronoun** is a word that takes the place of a noun.

Examples: I, you, he, she, it, we, they, my, mine, me, our, them

In the title of our story, there are three nouns:
"The **Cat**, the **Monkey**, and the **Chestnuts**"

If we replaced each noun with a pronoun, our silly title would look like this: "**She**, **He**, and **Them**"

It's a good thing we have nouns, so we know what we are talking about! Pronouns are important too; they keep our writing from sounding awkward.

Look at this sentence from our story, with all nouns and no pronouns: *Scarcely had the Cat touched the hot ashes than the Cat drew back with a cry, for the Cat had burned the Cat's paw.*

Now here it is again, with pronouns put back in: *Scarcely had the Cat touched the hot ashes than <u>she</u> drew back with a cry, for <u>she</u> had burned <u>her</u> paw.* It sounds much better!

The Cat, the Monkey and the Chestnuts
Vocabulary

Look up the following words in a dictionary and write down the meanings. Find the words in our story and circle them. Write a short sentence using one of the words.

1. hearth – <u>**the stone or brick floor of a fireplace; the**</u>

<u>**fireside**</u>

2. singed – <u>**to burn superficially or slightly**</u>

3. flatter – <u>**to praise insincerely**</u>

4. tempt – <u>**to entice to do something wrong**</u>

5. scarcely – <u>**hardly; not quite**</u>

Sentence: _____

The Cat, the Monkey and the Chestnuts
Pronouns

A <u>pronoun</u> is a word that takes the place of a noun.

In the following sentences from our story, find any pronouns, and name the nouns that they replace.

Example: "Your paws are, indeed, exactly like our master's hands."

Pronoun: _Your_ which replaces: _the Cat's_

Pronoun: _our_ which replaces: _the Cat and the Monkey's_

1. *She tried again, and made out to get one chestnut.*

Pronoun: **She** which replaces: ___the Cat___

2. *Then she pulled another, and a third.*

Pronoun: _she_ which replaces: ___the Cat___

3. *When she could pull no more, she turned, and found the Monkey had taken this time to crack the chestnuts and eat them.*

Pronoun: _she_ which replaces: ___the Cat___

Pronoun: _she_ which replaces: ___the Cat___

Pronoun: _them_ which replaces: _the chestnuts_

The Cat, the Monkey and the Chestnuts
Writing the Rough Draft

Read the story again. Write your rough draft of "The Cat, the Monkey and the Chestnuts." Tell the same story in your own words. When the Monkey speaks to the Cat, choose words that show that the Monkey is flattering the Cat in order to get the Cat to pull out the hot chestnuts for him. Show how hard it was for the Cat to pull the hot chestnuts out of the fire. Then write about the Monkey eating the nice warm chestnuts behind the Cat's back while she was doing all the work. When you are finished, read each sentence out loud to make sure it is a complete thought.

Edit your writing using the following checklist:

1. Spelling – all the words are spelled correctly. ⎯
2. Sentences –
   Each sentence expresses a complete thought. ⎯
   Each one has a subject and a verb. ⎯
3. Capitalization –
   All the important words in the title begin with capital letters. ⎯
   Every sentence begins with a capital letter. ⎯
   The word "I" is capitalized, if used. ⎯
   All proper names start with capital letters. ⎯
4. Punctuation –
   All of your sentences end with periods or exclamation marks. ⎯
   Any questions end with question marks. ⎯
5. Quotes –
   You have included at least one direct quote. ⎯
   You used quotation marks around the words spoken. ⎯

The Cat, the Monkey and the Chestnuts
Pronoun Practice

Circle all of the pronouns in the following passage from our previous story, "The Elves and the Shoemaker."

One evening, at Christmas-time, (he) and (his) (wife) sat over

the fire, chatting, and (he) said: "(I) should like to sit up and

watch to-night, that (we) may see who (it)'s that comes and

does (my) work for (me)." So (they) left the light burning, and

hid (themselves) behind a curtain to see what would happen.

*please note: "themselves" is a pronoun, but not one we have learned and therefore more difficult for the student to recognize

List five different pronouns that you found:

1. __he__   2. __I__

3. __we__   4. __it or themselves__

5. __my or they__

The Cat, the Monkey and the Chestnuts
Spelling Practice

Make a spelling list of up to five words you misspelled and had to correct in your original rough draft. Write each word correctly two times.

1. ____ __ANSWERS WILL VARY__

2. ____

3. ____

4. ____

5. ____

Now choose one of the words and use it in a sentence:

____

The Eight Parts of Speech

Fill in the top two right boxes with examples of different types of nouns and pronouns. Review the definition of a noun; memorize the definition of a pronoun.

Definitions	Examples
A **Noun** is a name for a person, place, thing or idea.	The student shall have listed several nouns here
A **Pronoun** is a word that takes the place of a noun.	and several pronouns here.

The Cat, the Monkey and the Chestnuts
Final Draft

Write your final draft. Now you may add some creative touches. Let's try to keep the basic story and events. You could change the main characters, the cat and the monkey, if you like, or you could name them. Remember that one should be cleverer than the other for the story to work. Use your imagination to add your own touches to the details.

Edit your writing using the following checklist:

1. Spelling – all the words are spelled correctly. ___
2. Sentences –
   Each sentence expresses a complete thought. ___
   Each one has a subject and a verb. ___
3. Capitalization –
   All the important words in the title begin with capital letters. ___
   Every sentence begins with a capital letter. ___
   The word "I" is capitalized, if used. ___
   All proper names start with capital letters. ___
4. Punctuation –
   All of your sentences end with periods or exclamation marks. ___
   Any questions end with question marks. ___
5. Quotes –
   You have included at least one direct quote. ___
   You used quotation marks around the words spoken. ___

Show your finished story to your teacher or parent.

123   Answer Key

How the Princess was Beaten in a Race
by Horace E. Scudder

There was once a king who had a daughter, and this daughter was very fair, so that every prince in all the countries around wished to marry her. Now the princess was a very swift runner. She ran so fast that no one could overtake her.

The king was in no haste to marry off his daughter, so he gave out that no one should have her for a wife who could not beat her in a race. Any one, prince or peasant, might race with her. The first man who beat her in the race should have her for wife; but whoever raced with her and did not beat must have his head cut off.

At first there were many who tried, for a great many princes were in love with her, and men who were not princes thought they might outstrip her, and so come to be as good as princes.

The girl had fine fun. She raced with each one, and she always beat in the game; a great many heads were cut off, and at last it was hard to find any one who dared to race with her. Now there was a poor young man in the country who thought thus to himself:

"I am poor, and have only my head to lose if I do not win the race. If I should win I should become noble, and all my family would be noble also. I think I will try."

He was a good runner, and he was also a fellow of quick wit. He heard that the princess was very fond of roses. So he gathered a fine nosegay. He also had a silken girdle made. Finally he took all his money and bought a silken bag, and placed in it a golden ball: on the ball were the words, "Who plays with me shall never tire of play."

These three things he placed in the bosom of his robe, and went and knocked at the palace gate. The porter asked him what he wished, and he said he had come to race with the princess. The princess herself, who was only a young girl, looked out of the window and heard what was said. She saw that he was poor and meanly clad, and she looked on him with scorn.

The Cat, the Monkey and the Chestnuts
More Pronouns

In each of the following sentences, circle all of the nouns. Then rewrite the sentence, replacing each noun with a pronoun.

Example: A (Cat) and a (Monkey) were sitting one day by the (hearth).
She and he were sitting one day by it.

1. The (Cat) and the (Monkey) were watching some (chestnuts) which their (master) had laid down to roast.

She and he (or they) were watching them which he had laid

down to roast.

2. The (Cat) was greatly flattered by this (speech).

She was greatly flattered by it.

3. The (Cat) reached forward for the tempting (chestnuts).

She reached forward for them.

4. The (Cat) had burned her paw.

She had burned it.

How the Princess was Beaten in a Race

Copywork

Copy the following sentences from our story. Make sure your sentences have correct capitals and punctuation.

She was near the goal, but the young man now let fall at her feet the silken bag. The ball of gold glittered in it, and the princess was curious to see what the plaything was.

Check that the student has copied the passage correctly. Check spelling, capital letters and punctuation.

But the king's law made no choice between rich and poor, prince and peasant. So the princess made ready to run. The king and all the court gathered to see the race, and the headsman went off to sharpen his axe.

The two had not run far, and the princess was outrunning the young man, when he drew forth his bunch of roses. He threw this so that it fell at the feet of the princess. She stopped, picked it up, and was greatly pleased with the flowers. She looked at them, smelled of them, and began to bind them in her hair. She forgot the race, when suddenly she saw the young man far ahead of her.

At once off she tore the roses, threw them from her, and ran like the wind. It was but a little while before she overtook the young man. She smote him lightly on the shoulder and said, "Stop, foolish boy! Do you hope to marry a princess?"

But as she sped past him, he threw before her the silken girdle. Again she stopped, and stooped to look at it. It was a beautiful girdle, and she clasped it about her waist. As she was buckling it, she saw the young man well on toward the goal.

"Wretch!" she cried, and burst into tears. Then she flung the girdle away and bounded forward. Once more she caught up with him. She seized him by the arm.

"You shall not marry me!" she said angrily, and sprang past him. She was near the goal, but the young man now let fall at her feet the silken bag. The ball of gold glittered in it, and the princess was curious to see what the plaything was. She paused for just a moment, raised the bag from the ground and took out the ball. It had letters on it, and she stood still to read them:

"Who plays with me shall never tire of play."

"I should like to see if that is true," said the princess, and she began to play with the ball. She tossed it and tossed it, and no one can say if she would have tired, for suddenly she heard a great shout. The young man had reached the winning-post: his head was safe. He married the princess, and all his family were made noble.

How the Princess was Beaten in a Race
Grammar Lesson – Verbs

MEMORIZE: A **verb** is a word that shows an action or a state of being.

There are two kinds of verbs we will learn about:

<u>Action Verbs</u> – An action verb is a word that shows an action, like *run, walk, eat, think, chew, study.*

Here's an easy test for action verbs: If you can put the word in the sentence, "**I can** _____," and it makes sense, then it is an action verb.
For example, "I can run." "I can walk." "I can think." "I can study."

<u>State-of-Being Verbs</u> – A state-of-being verb is a word that states that something *is*.
For example, "Melissa *is* smart." "Timothy *is* funny." "Kristen *is* beautiful." "He *was* tired." "They *were* in the pool." "I *am* happy."

You can remember the eight state-of-being verbs with a little chant. The rhythm goes like this:
slow, slow, quick-quick, slow, slow, slow, slow.
Now add the following words, in a sing-song voice:
is, am, were- was, are, be, being, been.

How the Princess was Beaten in a Race – Vocabulary

Look up the following words in a dictionary and write down the meanings. Find the words in our story and circle them. Write a short sentence using one of the words.

1. overtake – **to catch up with; to come upon suddenly**
   _____

2. girdle – **a belt for the waist**
   _____

3. clad – **clothed; dressed**
   _____

4. smote (look up "smite") – **to strike hard**
   _____

5. wit – **powers of thinking; mental faculties**
   _____

6. nosegay – **a small bunch of flowers**
   _____

Sentence: _____

How the Princess was Beaten in a Race
Writing the Rough Draft

Read the story again. Write your rough draft of "How the Princess was Beaten in a Race." Tell the same story in your own words. This is another long story - be sure to include each event. Choose words to describe what a fast runner the princess was. Describe each of the three things that the poor young boy brought with him when he came to the palace. Write about how frustrated the princess was to discover she had been tricked, and how happy the boy was to win the race and marry the princess. When you are finished, read each sentence out loud to make sure it is a complete thought.

Edit your writing using the following checklist:

1. Spelling - all the words are spelled correctly.
2. Sentences -
   Each sentence expresses a complete thought.
   Each one has a subject and a verb.
3. Capitalization -
   All the important words in the title begin with capital letters.
   Every sentence begins with a capital letter.
   The word "I" is capitalized, if used.
   All proper names start with capital letters.
4. Punctuation -
   All of your sentences end with periods or exclamation marks.
   Any questions end with question marks.
5. Quotes -
   You have included two or more direct quotes.
   You used quotation marks around the words spoken.
   You started a new line whenever a different character spoke.

How the Princess was Beaten in a Race
Verbs

Identify the following verbs as either action verbs (A) or state-of-being verbs (S). Remember our tests: action verbs can fit in the sentence "I can _____," and state-of-being verbs are sung in the chant.

1. **SB** were

2. **A** think

3. **A** race

4. **A** marry

5. **A** play

6. **SB** is

7. **SB** being

8. **A** run

9. **A** write

10. **SB** was

127   Answer Key

How the Princess was Beaten in a Race
Verb Practice

A **verb** is a word that shows an action or a state of being.
Circle all of the verbs in the following passage from our story:

He (was) a good runner, and he (was) also a fellow of quick

wit. He (heard) that the princess (was) very fond of roses.

So he (gathered) a fine nosegay. He also (had) a silken

girdle (made). Finally he (took) all his money and (bought) a

silken bag, and (placed) in it a golden ball; on the ball (were)

the words, "Who (plays) with me shall never (tire) of play."

These three things he (placed) in the bosom of his

robe, and (went) and (knocked) at the palace gate.

How the Princess was Beaten in a Race
Spelling Practice

Make a spelling list of up to five words you misspelled and had to correct in your original rough draft. Write each word correctly two times.

1. _____ **ANSWERS WILL VARY**

2. _____

3. _____

4. _____

5. _____

Now choose one of the words and use it in a sentence:

_____

_____

The Eight Parts of Speech

Fill in the top three right boxes with examples of different types of nouns, pronouns and verbs. Review the definitions of nouns and pronouns; memorize the definition of a verb.

Definitions	Examples
A **Noun** is a name for a person, place, thing or idea.	Check that the student has listed several nouns here,
A **Pronoun** is a word that takes the place of a noun.	several pronouns here,
A **Verb** is a word that shows an action or a state-of-being.	and several verbs here.

How the Princess was Beaten in a Race
Final Draft

Write your final draft. Now you may add some creative touches. Let's try to keep the basic story and events. You could change the main characters, the young man and the princess, or you could name the characters. You could change the items that the boy drops during the race to distract the princess. You could change the type of contest from a race to something else. Use your imagination to add your own touches to the details.

Edit your writing using the following checklist:

1. Spelling – all the words are spelled correctly. ____
2. Sentences –
   Each sentence expresses a complete thought. ____
   Each one has a subject and a verb. ____
3. Capitalization –
   All the important words in the title begin with capital letters. ____
   Every sentence begins with a capital letter. ____
   The word "I" is capitalized, if used. ____
   All proper names start with capital letters. ____
4. Punctuation –
   All of your sentences end with periods or exclamation marks. ____
   Any questions end with question marks. ____
5. Quotes –
   You have included two or more direct quotes. ____
   You used quotation marks around the words spoken. ____
   You started a new line whenever a different character spoke. ____

Show your finished story to your teacher or parent.

Answer Key

Cornelia's Jewels
by James Baldwin

It was a bright morning in the old city of Rome many hundred years ago. In a vine-covered summer-house in a beautiful garden, two boys were standing. They were looking at their mother and her friend, who were walking among the flowers and trees.

"Did you ever see so handsome a lady as our mother's friend?" asked the younger boy, holding his tall brother's hand. "She looks like a queen."

"Yet she is not so beautiful as our mother," said the elder boy. "She has a fine dress, it is true; but her face is not noble and kind. It is our mother who is like a queen."

"That is true," said the other. "There is no woman in Rome so much like a queen as our own dear mother."

Soon Cornelia, their mother, came down the walk to speak with them. She was simply dressed in a plain white robe. Her arms and feet were bare, as was the custom in those days; and no rings nor chains glittered about her hands and neck. For her only crown, long braids of soft brown hair were coiled about her head; and a tender smile lit up her noble face as she looked into her sons' proud eyes.

"Boys," she said, "I have something to tell you."

They bowed before her, as Roman lads were taught to do, and said, "What is it, mother?"

How the Princess was Beaten in a Race
Grammar Review

For each sentence:
(1) Circle all the beginning capitals in green.
(2) Circle all the end punctuation in red.
(3) Circle all the commas and quotation marks in blue.
(4) Circle all the nouns in purple.
(5) Circle all the pronouns in yellow.
(6) Circle all the verbs in orange.

1. The princess, who was only a girl, looked out of the window and heard the boy.

2. She saw that he was a peasant, and she looked at him with scorn.

3. At once she tore off the roses, threw them from her, and ran like the wind.

4. "Wretch!" she cried, and burst into tears.

Rewrite one of the above sentences as a question:
ANSWERS WILL VARY

_____

_____

Does your sentence start with a capital letter?

Answer Key   130

Cornelia's Jewels
Copywork

Copy the following sentences from our story. Make sure your sentences have correct capitals and punctuation.

In a vine-covered summer-house in a beautiful garden, two boys were standing. They were looking at their mother and her friend, who were walking among the flowers and trees.

Check that the student has copied the passage correctly. Check spelling, capital letters and punctuation.

"You are to dine with us to-day, here in the garden; and then our friend is going to show us that wonderful casket of jewels of which you have heard so much."

The brothers looked shyly at their mother's friend. Was it possible that she had still other rings besides those on her fingers? Could she have other gems besides those which sparkled in the chains about her neck?

When the simple outdoor meal was over, a servant brought the casket from the house. The lady opened it. Ah, how those jewels dazzled the eyes of the wondering boys! There were ropes of pearls, white as milk, and smooth as satin; heaps of shining rubies, red as the glowing coals; sapphires as blue as the sky that summer day; and diamonds that flashed and sparkled like the sunlight.

The brothers looked long at the gems. "Ah!" whispered the younger; "if our mother could only have such beautiful things!" At last, however, the casket was closed and carried carefully away.

"Is it true, Cornelia, that you have no jewels?" asked her friend. "Is it true, as I have heard it whispered, that you are poor?"

"No, I am not poor," answered Cornelia, and as she spoke she drew her two boys to her side; "for here are my jewels. They are worth more than all your gems."

I am sure that the boys never forgot their mother's pride and love and care; and in after years, when they had become great men in Rome, they often thought of this scene in the garden. And the world still likes to hear the story of Cornelia's jewels.

Cornelia's Jewels
Grammar Lesson – Adjectives

MEMORIZE: An <u>adjective</u> is a word that "decorates" a noun or a pronoun.

Adjectives add color to our writing!

Consider the first two sentences of "Cornelia's Jewels". First, let's read them without any adjectives:

It was morning in the city of Rome years ago. In a house in a garden, two boys were standing.

Now let's read them with the adjectives:

It was a bright morning in the old city of Rome many hundred years ago. In a vine-covered summer-house in a beautiful garden, two boys were standing.

Stories are much more interesting when they have adjectives added in. The reader can picture the scene just as the author intended, and will find the story much more enjoyable.

Cornelia's Jewels
Vocabulary

Look up the following words in a dictionary and write down the meanings. Find the words in our story and circle them. Write a short sentence using one of the words.

1. coil –<u>to wind into a circular or spiral form</u>

_____

2. gem <u>a precious stone, cut for use as a jewel</u>

_____

3. casket *(you will find at least two meanings for this word; be sure to pick the one that best fits our story)* –

<u>a small box or chest, as for valuables</u>

_____

_____

Sentence: _____

_____

Cornelia's Jewels
Adjectives

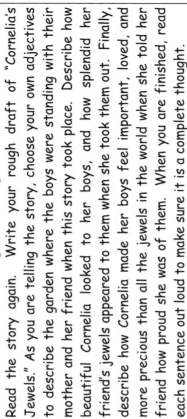

An **adjective** is a word that "decorates" a noun or a pronoun.

List two adjectives to describe Cornelia's clothes:

1. _____

   ANSWERS WILL VARY

2. _____

List three adjectives to describe the jewels in the casket:

1. _____

2. _____

3. _____

List two adjectives that the boys would use to describe their mother:

1. _____

2. _____

Cornelia's Jewels
Writing the Rough Draft

Read the story again. Write your rough draft of "Cornelia's Jewels." As you are telling the story, choose your own adjectives to describe the garden where the boys were standing with their mother and her friend when this story took place. Describe how beautiful Cornelia looked to her boys, and how splendid her friend's jewels appeared to them when she took them out. Finally, describe how Cornelia made her boys feel important, loved, and more precious than all the jewels in the world when she told her friend how proud she was of them. When you are finished, read each sentence out loud to make sure it is a complete thought.

Edit your writing using the following checklist:

1. Spelling – all the words are spelled correctly. ___
2. Sentences –
   Each sentence expresses a complete thought. ___
   Each one has a subject and a verb. ___
3. Capitalization –
   All the important words in the title begin with capital letters. ___
   Every sentence begins with a capital letter. ___
   The word "I" is capitalized, if used. ___
   All proper names start with capital letters. ___
4. Punctuation –
   All of your sentences end with periods or exclamation marks. ___
   Any questions end with question marks. ___
5. Quotes –
   You have included two or more direct quotes. ___
   You used quotation marks around the words spoken. ___
   You started a new line whenever a different character spoke. ___
6. Descriptions –
   You used adjectives to describe characters, places or things. ___

Answer Key

Cornelia's Jewels
Adjective Practice

An <u>adjective</u> is a word that "decorates" a noun or a pronoun.

Add adjectives to describe the nouns. Try to use different ones, to add interest.

Ah, how those jewels dazzled the eyes of the

_____ boys! There were ropes of

ANSWERS WILL VARY

_____ pearls, heaps of

_____ sapphires and

rubies, _____

_____ diamonds. The _____

brothers looked long at the _____

_____ gems.

Cornelia's Jewels
Spelling Practice

Make a spelling list of up to five words you misspelled and had to correct in your original rough draft. Write each word correctly two times.

1. _____

2. _____

ANSWERS WILL VARY

3. _____

4. _____

5. _____

Now choose one of the words and use it in a sentence:

_____

_____

The Eight Parts of Speech

Fill in the boxes on the right with examples of different types of nouns, pronouns, verbs and adjectives. Review the definitions of each one.

Definitions   *Examples*

A **Noun** is a name for a person, place, thing or idea.	Check that the student has written several nouns here,		
A **Pronoun** is a word that takes the place of a noun.	several pronouns here,		
A **Verb** is a word that shows an action or a state-of-being.	several verbs here,		
An **Adjective** is a word that decorates a noun or a pronoun.	and several adjectives here.		

Cornelia's Jewels
Final Draft

Write your final draft. Now you may add some creative touches. Let's try to keep the basic story and events. You could change the main characters, or you could name the brothers. You could change the precious items owned by the guest from jewels to something else. Use your imagination to add your own touches to the details.

Edit your writing using the following checklist:

1. Spelling – all the words are spelled correctly. ___
2. Sentences – ___
   Each sentence expresses a complete thought. ___
   Each one has a subject and a verb. ___
3. Capitalization – ___
   All the important words in the title begin with capital letters.
   Every sentence begins with a capital letter. ___
   The word "I" is capitalized, if used. ___
   All proper names start with capital letters. ___
4. Punctuation – ___
   All of your sentences end with periods or exclamation marks.
   Any questions end with question marks. ___
5. Quotes – ___
   You have included two or more direct quotes. ___
   You used quotation marks around the words spoken.
   You started a new line whenever a different character spoke. ___
6. Descriptions – ___
   You used adjectives to describe characters, places or things.

Show your finished story to your teacher or parent.

Answer Key

Alexander and Bucephalus
by James Baldwin

One day King Philip bought a fine horse called Bucephalus. He was a noble animal, and the king paid a very high price for him. But he was wild and savage, and no man could mount him, or do anything at all with him. They tried to whip him, but that only made him worse. At last the king bade his servants take him away.

"It is a pity to ruin so fine a horse as that," said Alexander, the king's young son. "Those men do not know how to treat him."

"Perhaps you can do better than they," said his father scornfully.

"I know," said Alexander, "that, if you would only give me leave to try, I could manage this horse better than any one else."

"And if you fail to do so, what then?" asked Philip.

"I will pay you the price of the horse," said the lad.

While everybody was laughing, Alexander ran up to Bucephalus, and turned his head toward the sun. He had noticed that the horse was afraid of his own shadow. He then spoke gently to the horse, and patted him with his hand. When he had quieted him a little, he made a quick spring, and leaped upon the horse's back.

Everybody expected to see the boy killed outright. But he kept his place, and let the horse run as fast as he would. By and by, when Bucephalus had become tired, Alexander reined him in, and rode back to the place where his father was standing.

Cornelia's Jewels
Grammar Review

Let's practice using pronouns and adjectives to make writing more interesting. Underline all of the nouns in the following passage. Replace *some* of them with pronouns. Add some adjectives in front of the nouns and pronouns. Then rewrite your finished product below.

When the simple outdoor meal was over, a

servant brought the casket from the house.

The lady opened it. Ah, how those jewels

dazzled the eyes of the wondering boys!

ANSWERS WILL VARY

Alexander and Bucephalus
Copywork

Copy the following sentences from our story. Make sure your sentences have correct capitals and punctuation.

One day King Philip bought a fine horse called Bucephalus. He was a noble animal, and the king paid a very high price for him. But he was wild and savage, and no man could mount him, or do anything at all with him.

Check that the student has copied the passage

correctly. Check spelling, capital letters

and punctuation.

All the men who were there shouted when they saw that the boy had proved himself to be the master of the horse. He leaped to the ground, and his father ran over and kissed him.

"My son," said the king, "Macedon is too small a place for you. You must seek a larger kingdom that will be worthy of you."

After that, Alexander and Bucephalus were the best of friends. They were said to be always together, for when one of them was seen, the other was sure to be not far away. But the horse would never allow any one to mount him but his master.

Alexander became the most famous king and warrior that was ever known; and for that reason he is always called Alexander the Great. Bucephalus carried him through many countries and in many fierce battles, and more than once did he save his master's life.

Alexander and Bucephalus
Grammar Lesson - Adverbs

MEMORIZE: An **adverb** is a word that "decorates" a verb.

Adverbs also add color to our writing, just like adjectives!

<u>Most</u> adverbs end in -ly. For example: He ran *quickly*. She gave money *generously*. Sally jumped *easily* over the creek. Few don't, such as *outside, tomorrow, there, then* or *more*.

Adverbs answer the questions, "When?" "Where?" , "How?" and "How much?"

For example, *When* did he run? He ran *recently*.
Where did he run? He ran *outside*.
How did he run? He ran *quickly*.
How much did he run? He ran *occasionally*.

Alexander and Bucephalus - Vocabulary

Look up the following words and write down the meanings. Find the words in our story and circle them. Write a short sentence using one of the words.

1. noble – **excellent, grand or stately**

_____

2. savage – **wild, uncultivated; fierce, untamed**

_____

3. scornfully – **to regard with great contempt**

_____

4. mount – **to climb up on something, as a horse**

_____

5. bade (look up *bid*, as a verb) – **to command or ask**

_____

Sentence: _____

_____

Alexander and Bucephalus
Writing the Rough Draft

Read the story again. Write your rough draft of "Alexander and Bucephalus." This story provides a great opportunity for you to find some exciting adjectives to show how wild the horse was and how brave Alexander was. Describe how exciting it was when Alexander rode the horse for the first time, and use important words at the end of your story when you describe what a great king Alexander eventually becomes. When you are finished, read each sentence out loud to make sure it is a complete thought.

Edit your writing using the following checklist:

1. Spelling – all the words are spelled correctly.
2. Sentences –
   Each sentence expresses a complete thought.
   Each one has a subject and a verb.
3. Capitalization –
   All the important words in the title begin with capital letters.
   Every sentence begins with a capital letter.
   The word "I" is capitalized, if used.
   All proper names start with capital letters.
4. Punctuation –
   All of your sentences end with periods or exclamation marks.
   Any questions end with question marks.
5. Quotes –
   You have included two or more direct quotes.
   You used quotation marks around the words spoken.
   You started a new line whenever a different character spoke.
6. Descriptions –
   You used adjectives to describe characters, places or things.

Alexander and Bucephalus
Adverbs

An **adverb** is a word that "decorates" a verb.

List two adverbs that could go in the blanks in the following sentences:

Bucephalus was wild and savage; he behaved _____.

1. __**ANSWERS WILL VARY**__

2. _____

While everybody was laughing, Alexander ran up to Bucephalus _____.

1. _____

2. _____

Circle the adverbs in the following sentences:

1. *"Perhaps you can do better than they," his father said scornfully.*

2. *He then spoke gently to the horse.*

Answer Key

Alexander and Bucephalus
Adverb Practice

An **<u>adverb</u>** is a word that "decorates" a verb.

Underline the adverb that tells *when:*

1. Bucephalus <u>never</u> allowed anyone to ride him.

2. The King's men <u>regularly</u> tried to whip Bucephalus into obedience.

Underline the adverb that tells *where:*

1. Alexander went <u>outside</u> to try to ride Bucephalus.

2. Bucephalus was running <u>here</u> in this field.

Underline the adverb that tells *how:*

1. Alexander spoke <u>gently</u> to the horse.

2. When Alexander had quieted him, he leaped <u>confidently</u> upon his back.

Underline the adverb that tells *how much:*

1. Bucephalus trusted Alexander <u>completely</u>.

2. Alexander <u>always</u> rode Bucephalus into battle.

Alexander and Bucephalus
Spelling Practice

Make a spelling list of up to five words you misspelled and had to correct in your original rough draft. Write each word correctly two times.

1. _____

2. _____   **ANSWERS WILL VARY**

3. _____

4. _____

5. _____

Now choose one of the words and use it in a sentence:

_____

_____

The Eight Parts of Speech

Fill in the boxes on the right with examples of different types of nouns, pronouns, verbs and adjectives. Review the definitions of each one.

Definitions	*Examples*
A **Noun** is a name for a person, place, thing or idea.	Check that the student has written several nouns here,
A **Pronoun** is a word that takes the place of a noun.	several pronouns here,
A **Verb** is a word that shows an action or a state-of-being.	several verbs here,
An **Adjective** is a word that decorates a noun or a pronoun.	several adjectives here,
An **Adverb** is a word that decorates a verb.	and several adverbs here.

Alexander and Bucephalus
Final Draft

Write your final draft. Now you may add some creative touches. Let's try to keep the basic story and events. Since this is a historical story, we need to keep the characters of Alexander and Bucephalus without changing them. You could add some detail about when Bucephalus first came home and the other men tried to ride him. Perhaps you may want to imagine what Alexander's first ride on Bucephalus was like. Use your imagination to make the story your own.

Edit your writing using the following checklist:

1. Spelling – all the words are spelled correctly. |
2. Sentences –
    Each sentence expresses a complete thought. |
    Each one has a subject and a verb. |
3. Capitalization –
    All the important words in the title begin with
    capital letters. |
    Every sentence begins with a capital letter. |
    The word "I" is capitalized, if used. |
    All proper names start with capital letters. |
4. Punctuation –
    All of your sentences end with periods or
    exclamation marks. |
    Any questions end with question marks. |
5. Quotes –
    You have included two or more direct quotes. |
    You used quotation marks around the words spoken. |
    You started a new line whenever a different character spoke. |
6. Descriptions –
    You used adjectives to describe characters, places or things. |

Show your finished story to your teacher or parent.

Answer Key

2. _____
   (adverb)   (verb)

3. _____
   (adverb)   (verb)

Rewrite the passage, replacing the adjectives with your own and adding your adverbs to the verbs.

_____

ANSWERS WILL VARY

_____

_____

_____

_____

_____

Alexander and Bucephalus
Grammar Review

Alexander was the most famous king and warrior that was ever known. Bucephalus carried him through many countries, and more than once did he save his master's life.

List two adjectives found in the above passage, and the nouns they describe:

1. __famous or most__ describes ___king___ .

2. ___many___ _____ describes ___countries___ .

List two adjectives that could be used instead of the ones in the passage:

1. _____   2. _____

ANSWERS WILL VARY

Underline all the verbs in the above passage. You should find at least three. List each one, and add an adverb to make it more interesting:

Answers will vary; verbs include *was, carried and save.*

1. _____
   (adverb)   (verb)

King Alfred and the Cakes
by James Baldwin

Many years ago there lived in England a wise and good king whose name was Alfred. No other man ever did so much for his country as he; and people now, all over the world, speak of him as Alfred the Great.

In those days a king did not have a very easy life. There was war almost all the time, and no one else could lead his army into battle so well as he. And so, between ruling and fighting, he had a busy time of it indeed.

A fierce, rude people, called the Danes, had come from over the sea, and were fighting the English. There were so many of them, and they were so bold and strong, that for a long time they gained every battle. If they kept on, they would soon be the masters of the whole country.

At last, after a great battle, the English army was broken up and scattered. Every man had to save himself in the best way he could. King Alfred fled alone, in great haste, through the woods and swamps.

Late in the day the king came to the hut of a woodcutter. He was very tired and hungry, and he begged the woodcutter's wife to give him something to eat and a place to sleep in her hut. The woman was baking some cakes upon the hearth, and she looked with pity upon the poor, ragged fellow who seemed so hungry. She had no thought that he was the king.

"Yes," she said, "I will give you some supper if you will watch these cakes. I want to go out and milk the cow; and you must see that they do not burn while I am gone."

King Alfred was very willing to watch the cakes, but he had far greater things to think about. How was he going to get his army together again? And how was he going to drive the fierce Danes out of the land? He forgot his hunger; he forgot the cakes; he forgot that he was in the woodcutter's hut. His mind was busy making plans for tomorrow.

In a little while the woman came back. The cakes were smoking on the hearth. They were burned to a crisp. Ah, how angry she was! "You lazy fellow!" she cried. "See what you have done! You want something to eat, but you do not want to work!" I have been told that she even struck the king with a stick; but I can hardly believe that she was so ill-natured.

The king must have laughed to himself at the thought of being scolded in this way and he was so hungry that he did not mind the woman's angry words half so much as the loss of the cakes.

I do not know whether he had anything to eat that night, or whether he had to go to bed without his supper. But it was not many days until he had gathered his men together again, and had beaten the Danes in a great battle.

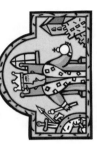

King Alfred and the Cakes
Vocabulary

Look up the following words and write down the meanings. Find the words in our story and circle them. Write a short sentence using one of the words.

1. fierce – <u>savage, violent</u>

2. scattered – <u>to separate and drive in many directions,</u>

<u>disperse</u>

3. haste – <u>quickness of motion; hurrying</u>

Sentence:

King Alfred and the Cakes
Copywork

Copy the following sentences from our story. Make sure your sentences have correct capitals and punctuation.

At last, after a great battle, the English army was broken up and scattered. Every man had to save himself in the best way he could. King Alfred fled alone, in great haste, through the woods and swamps.

Check that the student has copied the passage

correctly. Check spelling, capital letters

and punctuation.

King Alfred and the Cakes
Grammar Lesson - Prepositions

MEMORIZE: A **preposition** is a word that relates a noun or pronoun to other words in a sentence.

An easy way to identify a preposition is to ask if the word is something a squirrel can do to a tree! For example, the squirrel can go *near* the tree, *around* the tree, *over* the tree, *beside* the tree, *through* the tree (imagine the tree is hollow) and *under* the tree.

Memorize this song to the tune of "Yankee Doodle". It will help you remember 28 different prepositions.

Yankee Doodle Prepositions
Above, across, after, around,
    And then comes at;
Before, behind, below, beside,
    Between *and* by.
Down *and* during, for *and* from,
    In, inside *and* into;
Of, off, on, out, over, through,
    To, under, up *and* with!

King Alfred and the Cakes
Prepositions

A **preposition** is a word that relates a noun or pronoun to other words in a sentence.

Circle the prepositions in each sentence. Use "Yankee Doodle Prepositions" to help you. Two of the sentences contain more than one preposition.

1. *(In) those days a king did not have a very easy life.*

2. *The Danes had come (from) (over) the sea.*

3. *They would soon be masters (of) the whole country.*

4. *The king came (to) the hut (of) a woodcutter.*

5. *The woman was baking some cakes (on) the hearth.*

6. *His mind was busy making plans (for) tomorrow.*

In sentence 3, can you find the adverb that tells "when?"

_____ soon

145   Answer Key

King Alfred and the Cakes
Spelling Practice

Make a spelling list of up to five words you misspelled and had to correct in your original rough draft. Write each word correctly two times.

ANSWERS WILL VARY

1. _____ _____

2. _____ _____

3. _____ _____

4. _____ _____

5. _____ _____

Now choose one of the words and use it in a sentence:

_____

_____

King Alfred and the Cakes
Writing the Rough Draft

Read the story again. Write your rough draft of "King Alfred and the Cakes." Be sure to include in the beginning of your story what a good king he was, and what a hard time he was having fighting the fierce, rude Danes. Describe how hungry he was when he arrived at the woodcutter's hut, and how ragged he looked after days in battle. And don't forget how angry the wife was when the king let her cakes burn! When you are finished, read each sentence out loud to make sure it is a complete thought.

Edit your writing using the following checklist:

1. Spelling – all the words are spelled correctly. ___
2. Sentences –
   Each sentence expresses a complete thought. ___
   Each one has a subject and a verb. ___
3. Capitalization –
   All the important words in the title begin with capital letters. ___
   Every sentence begins with a capital letter. ___
   The word "I" is capitalized, if used. ___
   All proper names start with capital letters. ___
4. Punctuation –
   All of your sentences end with periods or exclamation marks. ___
   Any questions end with question marks. ___
5. Quotes –
   You have included two or more direct quotes. ___
   You used quotation marks around the words spoken. ___
   You started a new line whenever a different character spoke. ___
6. Descriptions –
   You used adjectives to describe characters, places or things. ___

King Alfred and the Cakes
Final Draft

Write your final draft. Now you may add some creative touches. Let's try to keep the basic story and events. Since this is a historical story, we need to keep the character of King Alfred without too many changes. You could add some detail about the woman in the hut. Why was she so busy? What prompted her to offer hospitality to the ragged man who appeared at her door? What kind of battle plans did the King make while the cakes were burning? Use your imagination to make the story your own.

Edit your writing using the following checklist:

1. Spelling – all the words are spelled correctly. ⎯⎯
2. Sentences – ⎯⎯
   Each sentence expresses a complete thought. ⎯⎯
   Each one has a subject and a verb.
3. Capitalization –
   All the important words in the title begin with ⎯⎯
   capital letters.
   Every sentence begins with a capital letter. ⎯⎯
   The word "I" is capitalized, if used. ⎯⎯
   All proper names start with capital letters. ⎯⎯
4. Punctuation –
   All of your sentences end with periods or ⎯⎯
   exclamation marks.
   Any questions end with question marks. ⎯⎯
5. Quotes –
   You have included two or more direct quotes. ⎯⎯
   You used quotation marks around the words spoken. ⎯⎯
   You started a new line whenever a different character spoke. ⎯⎯
6. Descriptions –
   You used adjectives to describe characters, places or things. ⎯⎯

Show your finished story to your teacher or parent.

King Alfred and the Cakes
Preposition Practice

A **preposition** is a word that relates a noun or pronoun to other words in a sentence.

List 15 prepositions. You may use the "Yankee Doodle Prepositions" song to help you.

1. _____   2. _____   3. _____

4. _____   5. _____   6. _____

CHECK THAT ALL ANSWERS ARE PREPOSITIONS

7. _____   8. _____   9. _____

10. _____   11. _____   12. _____

13. _____   14. _____   15. _____

Write a command sentence that might have been in the story, using one of your prepositions.

ANSWERS WILL VARY

_____

Write a question about the story and include one of your prepositions.

ANSWERS WILL VARY

_____

147

Answer Key

King Alfred and the Cakes
Grammar Review

The king must have <u>laughed</u> to himself at the <u>thought</u> of being <u>scolded</u> in this way; and he was so <u>hungry</u> that he did not mind the <u>woman's</u> angry words half so much as the loss of the <u>cakes</u>.

ANSWERS WILL VARY

List a noun that could replace *king*: _____

List a verb that could replace *laughed*: _____

List a noun that could replace *thought*: _____

List an adverb that could replace *scolded*: _____

List an adjective that could replace *hungry*: _____

List a noun that could replace *woman*: _____

List a noun that could replace *cakes*: _____

The Eight Parts of Speech

Fill in the boxes on the right with examples of different types of nouns, pronouns, verbs, adjectives, adverbs and prepositions. Review the definitions of each one.

Definitions	Examples
A **Noun** is a name for a person, place, thing or idea.	Check that the student has written several nouns here,
A **Pronoun** is a word that takes the place of a noun.	several pronouns here,
A **Verb** is a word that shows an action or a state-of-being.	several verbs here,
An **Adjective** is a word that decorates a noun or a pronoun.	several adjectives here,
An **Adverb** is a word that decorates a verb.	several adverbs here,
A **Preposition** is a word that relates a noun or a pronoun to other words in a sentence.	and several prepositions here.

The Travels of Ching
by Robert Bright

In the land of China a dollmaker made a little doll. The doll's name was Ching. The dollmaker stuffed Ching with the best stuffing and glued him with the best glue. He sewed him up with the best thread. Then he sold him.

He sold Ching to a toy shop where everything was very expensive. For a long time Ching sat in the toy shop and waited. He was waiting for someone who wanted him.

Now there was a little Chinese girl who came by the toy shop. This little girl wanted Ching. But she was poor. She wanted to have Ching more than anything, but she had no money to buy him.

So Ching was sold to a rich tea merchant who drove away with him in his rickshaw. But the tea merchant did not want Ching for himself. He took Ching to the post office and sent him far, far away.

He sent Ching down a mountain on a donkey...
and down a river in a sailboat...
and across the ocean on a steamship...
all the way to America...
and on across America to a city...
where the postman delivered Ching...
to a little girl who lived in a beautiful penthouse.

Fill in your replacement words to create a new way to tell the same story:

ANSWERS WILL VARY

The _____ must have _____ of being _____ to himself at the _____

_____ in this way; and he was so _____

_____ that he did not mind the _____

_____ 's angry words half so much

as the loss of the _____.

But the little girl did not want Ching. She already had more dolls and dresses and things than she knew what to do with. She took Ching out on the terrace and left him sitting on the edge. It was a careless thing to have done.

Ching fell off. Luckily he floated. He landed in a small tree in a small back yard – and hung there. Then he dropped into a flower bed – and sat there. When it rained Ching got wet. When it snowed Ching got cold.

At last, in the Spring, an old gentleman found him sitting in the flower bed. He was a nice old gentleman and took Ching inside. But the old gentleman did not want Ching. What *he* liked was old chairs and old tables and old pieces of bric-a-brac. He did not care for a dirty doll.

So the old gentleman gave Ching to his cook. But the cook did not want Ching. Her kitchen was very neat and she did not want it cluttered. She threw Ching into the rubbish can.

Many people went by. But nobody wanted Ching. He was too dirty.

Early in the morning the rubbish man came and dumped Ching into his truck. But the rubbish man did not want Ching; what he wanted was old bones and old rags and old paper and old tin cans. The rubbish man took Ching to his rubbish yard but he had to put him in a separate place all by himself.

One day a Chinese laundry man came by and bought Ching. All the rubbish man charged for him was fifteen cents. Imagine! The laundry man took Ching to his laundry and combed his hair. He washed his robe and ironed it. He went to a lot of trouble.

But the laundry man did not want Ching. He only bought him to give away to somebody else. He took Ching to the post office and sent him far, far away.

He sent Ching across America on a train...
and across the ocean on a ship...
and up a river on a sailboat...
and up a mountain on a donkey...
all the way to his little niece in China.

And this little girl DID want Ching!

She had always wanted Ching more than anything else, since she saw him in the toy shop. Do you remember?

She put him into her cart and took him for a nice ride over her favorite bridge. And in the evening she and Ching had supper together in the cozy kitchen. Then they went to bed. They lay in bed together right next to each other.

Outside a wise old Chinese owl looked in and the moon shone. The cat slept on the window sill.

The little girl put her arm around Ching because she was so glad to have him.

The Travels of Ching – Vocabulary

Look up the following words and write down the meanings. Find the words in our story and circle them. Write a short sentence using one of the words.

1. rickshaw – a small covered 2-wheeled vehicle usually for one passenger that is pulled by one man and that was used originally in Japan

2. merchant – storekeeper; the operator of a retail business

3. bric-a-brac – a miscellaneous collection of small articles commonly of ornamental or sentimental value

4. penthouse – a house or apartment on the roof of a building

5. terrace – an unroofed, paved area next to a house and overlooking a garden

6. rubbish – any material thrown away as useless; trash

Sentence: _____

The Travels of Ching
Copywork

Copy the following sentences from our story. Make sure your sentences have correct capitals and punctuation.

Outside a wise old Chinese owl looked in and the moon shone. The cat slept on the window sill. The little girl put her arm around Ching because she was so glad to have him.

Check that the student has copied the passage correctly. Check spelling, capital letters and punctuation.

---

151   Answer Key

The Travels of Ching
Conjunctions

A **conjunction** is a joining word that connects words or phrases together.

Circle the conjunctions "and" or "but" in each sentence.

1. The dollmaker stuffed Ching with the best stuffing (and) glued him with the best glue.

2. For a long time Ching sat in the toy shop (and) waited.

3. She wanted to have Ching more than anything, (but) she had no money to buy him.

4. He sent Ching down a mountain on a donkey (and) down a river in a sailboat (and) across the ocean on a steamship all the way to America (and) on across America to a city where the postman delivered Ching to a little girl who lived in a beautiful penthouse.

5. She already had more dolls (and) dresses (and) things than she knew what to do with.

In sentence 4, can you find two adjectives?

little   beautiful

The Travels of Ching
Grammar Lesson – Conjunctions

MEMORIZE: A **conjunction** is a joining word that connects words or phrases together.

The most popular conjunction is the word "and."

"And" is as powerful as super-glue!

It can connect words, like "bat *and* ball," "milk *and* cookies," or "King Alfred *and* the Cakes."

It can also connect phrases. "She took Ching out on the terrace *and* left him sitting on the edge." "One day a Chinese laundry man came by *and* bought Ching."

The word "*and*" can even connect sentences: "Outside a wise old Chinese owl looked in *and* the moon shone."

Other popular conjunctions are "*but*" and "*or*." "The rubbish man took Ching to his rubbish yard *but* he had to put him in a separate place." "Ching did not find a home at the tea merchants *or* hanging in the tree *or* in the rubbish can."

Other words that can be used as conjunctions are "after," "until," "therefore," or "however."

The Travels of Ching
Spelling Practice

Make a spelling list of up to five words you misspelled and had to correct in your original rough draft. Write each word correctly two times.

1. _____ _____

2. _____ _____

   ANSWERS WILL VARY

3. _____ _____

4. _____ _____

5. _____ _____

Now choose one of the words and use it in a sentence:

_____

_____

The Travels of Ching
Writing the Rough Draft

Read the story again. Write your rough draft of "The Travels of Ching." Can you remember all the places Ching went on his travels? Be sure to include each of Ching's adventures, and at the end of your story, show how happy the little girl was to finally receive Ching for her very own. When you are finished, read each sentence out loud to make sure it is a complete thought.

Edit your writing using the following checklist:

1. Spelling – all the words are spelled correctly. ____

2. Sentences –
   Each sentence expresses a complete thought. ____
   Each one has a subject and a verb. ____

3. Capitalization –
   All the important words in the title begin with capital letters. ____
   Every sentence begins with a capital letter. ____
   The word "I" is capitalized, if used. ____
   All proper names start with capital letters. ____

4. Punctuation –
   All of your sentences end with periods or exclamation marks. ____
   Any questions end with question marks. ____

5. Quotes –
   You have included two or more direct quotes. ____
   You used quotation marks around the words spoken. ____
   You started a new line whenever a different character spoke. ____

6. Descriptions –
   Describe where your story takes place. ____
   Describe what your characters look like. ____
   Describe what your characters feel. ____

Answer Key

The Travels of Ching
Final Draft

Write your final draft. Now you may add some creative touches. Let's try to keep the basic story and events. Make it your very own story by adding some adjectives and adverbs. You could add some more descriptive words to Ching when the toymaker is making him. Describe the rich little girl who didn't want Ching. You could describe the winter when Ching is sitting in the flower bed. How did the old gentleman find him? Or describe how Ching looked when the laundry man decided to buy him. You could use your imagination towards the end of the story to tell us more about the little girl who ended up with Ching and loved him so much. You decide what will be best for your story!

Edit your writing using the following checklist:

1. Spelling – all the words are spelled correctly.
2. Sentences –
   Each sentence expresses a complete thought.
   Each one has a subject and a verb.
3. Capitalization –
   All the important words in the title begin with capital letters.
   Every sentence begins with a capital letter.
   The word "I" is capitalized, if used.
   All proper names start with capital letters.
4. Punctuation –
   All of your sentences end with periods or exclamation marks.
   Any questions end with question marks.

The Travels of Ching
Conjunction Practice

A **conjunction** is a joining word that connects words or phrases together.

List 4 conjunctions. **Answers will vary but should include "and," "but," "or." May also include "therefore," "until" or "however."**

1. _____ 2. _____

3. _____ 4. _____

Write a question that might have been in the story, using one of your conjunctions.

ANSWERS WILL VARY

Write a statement about the story and include a conjunction.

How many times is the word "and" used in our story? **31**

Find two words that "and" is used to connect:
ANSWERS WILL VARY

The Eight Parts of Speech

Fill in the boxes on the right with examples of different types of nouns, pronouns, verbs, adjectives, adverbs, prepositions and conjunctions. Review the definitions of each one.

Definitions	Examples
A **Noun** is a name for a person, place, thing or idea.	**Check that the student has written several nouns here,**
A **Pronoun** is a word that takes the place of a noun.	several pronouns here,
A **Verb** is a word that shows an action or a state-of-being.	several verbs here,
An **Adjective** is a word that decorates a noun or a pronoun.	several adjectives here,
An **Adverb** is a word that decorates a verb.	several adverbs here,
A **Preposition** is a word that relates a noun or a pronoun to other words in a sentence.	several prepositions here,
A **Conjunction** is a joining word that connects words or phrases together.	and several conjunctions here.

---

5. Quotes –
   You have included two or more direct quotes. ___
   You used quotation marks around the words spoken. ___
   You started a new line whenever a different character spoke. ___

6. Descriptions –
   Describe where your story takes place. ___
   Describe what your characters look like. ___
   Describe what your characters feel. ___

Show your finished story to your teacher or parent.

Answer Key

King Canute on the Seashore
by James Baldwin

A hundred years or more after the time of Alfred the Great there was a king of England named Canute. King Canute was a Dane, but the Danes were not so fierce and cruel then as they had been when they were at war with King Alfred.

The great men and officers who were around King Canute were always praising him, "You are the greatest man that ever lived," one would say. Then another would say, "O king! there can never be another man so mighty as you." And another would say, "Great Canute, there is nothing in the world that dares to disobey you." The king was a man of sense, and he grew very tired of hearing such foolish speeches.

One day he was by the seashore, and his officers were with him. They were praising him, as they were in the habit of doing. He thought that now he would teach them a lesson, and so he bade them set his chair on the beach close by the edge of the water.

"Am I the greatest man in the world?" he asked.

"O king!" they cried, "There is no one so mighty as you."

"Do all things obey me?" he asked.

"There is nothing that dares to disobey you, O king!" they said. "The world bows before you, and gives you honor."

The Travels of Ching
Grammar Review

The little girl wanted to have Ching more than anything, but she had no money to buy him. So Ching was sold to a rich tea merchant who drove away with him in his rickshaw.

List the two phrases that are connected by the word "but":

The little girl wanted to have Ching more than anything."", "she had no money to buy him."

List an adjective that could replace "little": _____

List two adjectives that could replace "rich" and "tea":
ANSWERS WILL VARY
_____   _____

List an adverb that could describe how the merchant

drove away in his rickshaw: _____

King Canute on the Seashore
Copywork

Copy the following sentences from our story. Make sure your sentences have correct capitals and punctuation.

"There is only one King who is all-powerful: and it is He who rules the sea, and holds the ocean in the hollow of His hand. It is He whom you ought to praise and serve above all others."

Check that the student has copied the passage correctly. Check spelling, capital letters and punctuation.

"Will the sea obey me?" he asked; and he looked down at the little waves which were lapping the sand at his feet.

The foolish officers were puzzled, but they did not dare to say, "Oh, no." "Command it, O king! And it will obey," said one.

"Sea," cried Canute, "I command you to come no farther! Waves, stop your rolling, and do not dare to touch my feet!"

But the tide came in, just as it always did. The water rose higher and higher. It came up around the king's chair, and wet not only his feet, but also his robe. His officers stood about him, alarmed, and wondering whether he was not mad.

Then Canute took off his crown, and threw it down upon the sand. "I shall never wear it again," he said. "And do you, my men, learn a lesson from what you have seen. There is only one King who is all-powerful: and it is He who rules the sea, and holds the ocean in the hollow of His hand. It is He whom you ought to praise and serve above all others."

Answer Key

King Canute on the Seashore
Grammar Lesson - Interjections

MEMORIZE: An **interjection** is a word or phrase that expresses surprise or emotion.

Interjections are usually followed by either commas or exclamation points.

Hey, what's the king doing?

Wow! The king's going to get wet!

Oh no! The tide is coming in!

O king, you are the greatest.

Here are some examples of other common interjections:

Hooray!
Alas.
Unreal!
Oh!
Ah!
Hmmm.
Whoops!

King Canute on the Seashore
Vocabulary

Look up the following words and write down the meanings. Find the words in our story and circle them. Write a short sentence using one of the words.

1. bade *(verb, past tense, look up "bid")* – **to command or**

   ask

2. lap *(verb)* – **to strike gently with a light splash**

3. mad *(find a definition that does **not** mean "angry")* –

   mentally ill; foolish and rash

Sentence: _____

King Canute on the Seashore
Writing the Rough Draft

Read the story again. Write your rough draft of "King Canute on the Seashore." Tell how the king's officers praised him all the time. Describe the beach where the story takes place. Describe how the tide came up little by little, and dared to touch the king's robe, despite his command not to do so! Choose words for King Canute's final speech that sound as if they are meant to teach the officers a lesson about which King truly is the most powerful. When you are finished, read each sentence out loud to make sure it is a complete thought.

Edit your writing using the following checklist:

1. Spelling – all the words are spelled correctly. | —
2. Sentences –
   Each sentence expresses a complete thought. | —
   Each one has a subject and a verb. | —
3. Capitalization –
   All the important words in the title begin with capital letters. | —
   Every sentence begins with a capital letter. | —
   The word "I" is capitalized, if used. | —
   All proper names start with capital letters. | —
4. Punctuation –
   All of your sentences end with periods or exclamation marks. | —
   Any questions end with question marks. | —
5. Quotes –
   You have included two or more direct quotes. | —
   You used quotation marks around the words spoken. | —
   You started a new line whenever a different character spoke. | —
6. Descriptions –
   Describe where your story takes place. | —
   Describe what your characters look like. | —
   Describe what your characters feel. | —

King Canute on the Seashore
Interjections

An <u>interjection</u> is a word or phrase that expresses surprise or emotion.

There is a two-word interjection that occurs several times in our story. Can you find it?

<u>O</u>   <u>king</u>

What might be some interjections that the king could have said when the sea came up around his chair?
ANSWERS WILL VARY -could include "Yikes", "Oh no"

What could the soldiers have said when they were watching the sea come up around the king?
ANSWERS WILL VARY -could include "Help", "Wow"

Write a sentence about our story using an interjection:
ANSWERS WILL VARY

159   Answer Key

King Canute on the Seashore
Interjection Practice

An <u>interjection</u> is a word or phrase that expresses surprise or emotion.

Circle the interjection that best fits each sentence.

1. _____, King Canute lived a long time ago!
   a. (Wow)   b. Surprise   c. Ouch

2. "_____, you are the greatest man that ever lived."
   a. Alas   b. (King)   c. Unreal

3. "_____! Our king is the best!"
   a. (Hooray)   b. Whoops   c. Oh

4. "_____? Will the sea obey me?"
   a. Excellent   b. Alas   c. (Really)

5. "_____! I command you not to come any closer!"
   a. Hmmm   b. Excellent   c. (No)

6. _____! The king is standing in the water!
   a. (Oh no)   b. Hooray   c. Right

7. _____, the king's officers should learn that only one King in heaven can control the sea.
   a. OK   b. (Alas)   c. Great

King Canute on the Seashore
Spelling Practice

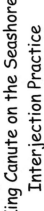

Make a spelling list of up to five words you misspelled and had to correct in your original rough draft. Write each word correctly two times.

1. _____

2. _____

ANSWERS WILL VARY

3. _____

4. _____

5. _____

Now choose one of the words and use it in a sentence:

_____

_____

The Eight Parts of Speech

Fill in the boxes on the right with examples of different types of nouns, pronouns, verbs, adjectives, adverbs, prepositions and conjunctions. Review the definitions of each one.

Definitions	Examples
A **Noun** is a name for a person, place, thing or idea.	Check that the student has written several nouns here,
A **Pronoun** is a word that takes the place of a noun.	several pronouns here,
A **Verb** is a word that shows an action or a state-of-being.	several verbs here,
An **Adjective** is a word that decorates a noun or a pronoun.	several adjectives here,
An **Adverb** is a word that decorates a verb.	several adverbs here,
A **Preposition** is a word that relates a noun or a pronoun to other words in a sentence.	several prepositions here,
A **Conjunction** is a joining word that connects words or phrases together.	several conjunctions here,
An **Interjection** is a word or phrase that expresses surprise or emotion.	and several interjections here.

King Canute on the Seashore
Final Draft

Write your final draft. Now you may add some creative touches. Let's try to keep the basic story and events. Make it your very own story by adding some adjectives and adverbs. You could add some more descriptive words to the king's officers. Describe King Canute. Why are they all by the beach? How did the officers react when they thought King Canute was crazy? What did they do when King Canute said at the end of the story that he would never wear a crown again? Use your imagination!

Edit your writing using the following checklist:

1. Spelling - all the words are spelled correctly. ___
2. Sentences -
   Each sentence expresses a complete thought. ___
   Each one has a subject and a verb. ___
3. Capitalization -
   All the important words in the title begin with capital letters. ___
   Every sentence begins with a capital letter. ___
   The word "I" is capitalized, if used. ___
   All proper names start with capital letters. ___
4. Punctuation -
   All of your sentences end with periods or exclamation marks. ___
   Any questions end with question marks. ___
5. Quotes -
   You have included two or more direct quotes. ___
   You used quotation marks around the words spoken. ___
   You started a new line whenever a different character spoke. ___
6. Descriptions -
   Describe where your story takes place. ___
   Describe what your characters look like. ___
   Describe what your characters feel. ___

Show your finished story to your teacher or parent.

The Three Goats Named Bruse
by James Baldwin

Three goats once lived together on a mountain, and every one of them was named Bruse. It was hard for them to find enough to eat, for there were no trees there, and only a few blades of grass grew among the cracks and crevices of the rocks.

"What a fine pasture that must be on the other mountain beyond the waterfall!" said the great goat Bruse one morning.

"Yes," said his brother, the second goat Bruse, "you can see the green grass plainly. It makes my mouth water only to look at it; and it is all going to waste, for there is not a goat there to eat it."

"I mean to get my dinner there this very day," said the little goat Bruse; and he held his head very high.

"So will we, little brother," said the other two goats. "But since you cannot eat as fast as we can, you may go first, and we will follow after."

Now, the only way by which they could reach the other mountain was to cross a high bridge over the waterfall. Under this bridge, among the rocks and the spray, there lived a great ugly fairy called a Troll, with eyes as big as frying pans and a nose as long as a broomstick. But the little goat Bruse knew nothing about the Troll; he only saw the green grass on the side of the mountain, and he never thought of any danger on the way. When he came to the bridge he looked neither to the right nor to the left, but walked bravely along.

"Trip trap, trip trap, trip trap," said the bridge, as he went over.
"Who trips on my bridge?" cried the Troll.
"Oh, it's only the little goat Bruse. I am going over to the other mountain to get my dinner and grow fat," said the goat, in a soft voice.
"No, you won't," said the Troll, "for I am going to eat you up," and he began to stir from his place by the side of the waterfall.
"Oh! Now, please don't hurt me, for I am so little," said the goat; "but if you will wait a while, the second goat Bruse will soon come this way and he is much bigger."
"Very well," said the Troll; "you may pass."

King Canute on the Seashore
Grammar Review

But the tide came in, just as it always did. The water rose *higher* and higher. It came up around the king's chair, *and* and wet not only his *feet*, *but* also his robe. His officers stood about him, *alarmed*, *and* *wondering* whether he was not mad.

Find six nouns in the above passage:

1. tide   2. water   3. chair

4. feet   5. robe   6. officers

Find three pronouns:

3 of the following: it   his   him   he

1. _____   2. _____   3. _____

Find an adverb that describes how the water rose: **higher**

List two adjectives that describe the officers: *check that four of the five are circled.*

1. **alarmed**   2. **wondering**

Find and circle four conjunctions in the passage. *check that four of the five are circled.*

The Three Goats Named Bruse
Copywork

Copy the following sentences from our story. Make sure your sentences have correct capitals and punctuation.

"Now, the only way by which they could reach the other mountain was to cross a high bridge over the waterfall. Under this bridge, among the rocks and the spray, there lived a great ugly fairy called a Troll, with eyes as big as frying pans and a nose as long as a broomstick."

Check that the student has copied the passage correctly. Check spelling, capital letters and punctuation.

In about an hour the second goat Bruse came down to cross the bridge. He held his head up very high, and looked neither to the right nor to the left.

"Trap trap, trap trap, trap trap," said the bridge.

"Who is it that trap-traps over my bridge?" asked the Troll.

"Oh, it is only the second goat Bruse. I am going across to the other mountain to eat grass and grow fat," said the goat, trying to make his harsh voice sound weak and piping.

"No, you are not," said the Troll, "for I am going to eat you up," and he made a great noise in the water about him.

"Oh! Please don't," said the goat, "for I would hardly make you a good mouthful. Wait a little while, and then the great goat Bruse will come this way; he is ever so much bigger than I am."

"Very well," said the Troll; "you may pass."

In a few minutes the great goat Bruse came down, and walked boldly upon the bridge.

"Trap trop, trap trop, trap trop—ah!" said the bridge. For the goat was so heavy that the boards creaked and cracked under him.

"Who goes tramping on my bridge?" cried the Troll.

"It is I, the great goat Bruse," said the goat, in a very coarse tone of voice. "I am going over to the other mountain to eat up all your grass."

"No, you are not," said the Troll, making a great stir in the waterfall: "for it is I that am going to eat you. I am after you now!"

"Well, then, come on," said the goat, "and I'll give you a taste of my two spears."

And as soon as the Troll lifted his head above the sides of the bridge, the great goat Bruse rushed upon him, and thrust out his eyes with his horns, and broke his bones, and tossed him back into the deep, cold water below. Then he went on, over to the other mountain.

The three goats named Bruse found more green grass than they could eat in many a day, and they grew so fat that they never cared to cross the bridge over the waterfall again. And if they have not lost their fat, they are still as fat as ever.

Answer Key

The Three Goats Named Bruse
Grammar Review – Types of Sentences

Label each sentence as a statement (S), question (Q), and command (C) or exclamation (E).

1. __S__ Three goats once lived together on a mountain.

2. __E__ They were very hungry! *(S could also be correct)*

3. __Q__ "Can you see the green grass on the other mountain?"

4. __S__ Under the bridge there lived a great ugly Troll.

5. __C__ "Don't hurt me, for I am so little."

6. __Q__ "Who is it that trap-traps over my bridge?"

7. __S__ In a few minutes the great goat Bruse came down, and walked boldly upon the bridge.

8. __E__ "Look out!"

9. __C__ Go and see the three fat goats up on the mountain.

The Three Goats Named Bruse
Vocabulary

Look up the following words and write down the meanings. Find the words in our story and circle them. Then write a short sentence using one of the words.

1. crevice - __a narrow opening caused by a crack or split__

2. spray *(hint: find a noun that has something to do with water)* - __a mist of fine liquid particles__

3. piping - __to make shrill sounds; to utter shrilly__

4. coarse - __rough, harsh__

5. spears - __weapons with long shafts and sharp heads for thrusting__

Sentence: _____

The Three Goats Named Bruse
Spelling Practice

Make a spelling list of up to five words you misspelled and had to correct in your original rough draft. Write each word correctly two times.

1. _____

2. _____ **ANSWERS WILL VARY**

3. _____

4. _____

5. _____

Now choose one of the words and use it in a sentence:

_____

_____

The Three Goats Named Bruse
Writing the Rough Draft

Read the story again. Write your rough draft of "The Three Goats Named Bruse." Describe the first pasture where the goats lived, and the high bridge over the waterfall they needed to cross in order to reach the greener grass on the other side. Describe the size of each goat and the different sounds they made as they walked across the bridge. And make the encounter with the Troll exciting for your reader! When you are finished, read each sentence out loud to make sure it is a complete thought.

Edit your writing using the following checklist:

1. Spelling – all the words are spelled correctly. ____
2. Sentences –
   Each sentence expresses a complete thought. ____
   Each one has a subject and a verb. ____
3. Capitalization –
   All the important words in the title begin with capital letters. ____
   Every sentence begins with a capital letter. ____
   The word "I" is capitalized, if used. ____
   All proper names start with capital letters. ____
4. Punctuation –
   All of your sentences end with periods or exclamation marks. ____
   Any questions end with question marks. ____
5. Quotes –
   You have included two or more direct quotes. ____
   You used quotation marks around the words spoken. ____
   You started a new line whenever a different character spoke. ____
6. Descriptions –
   Describe where your story takes place. ____
   Describe what your characters look like. ____
   Describe what your characters feel. ____
   Use adverbs to describe how your characters might have acted. ____

Parts of Speech Crossword Puzzle

Student Page 167 – Lesson 28

Write the correct part of speech for each definition in the puzzle.

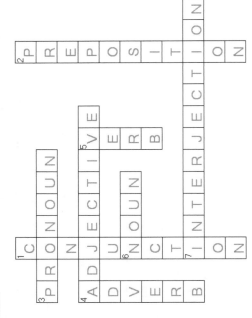

Crossword answers:
- C
- ³P R O N O U N
- ²P R E P O S I T I O N
- A D J E C T I V E
- E
- D U
- ⁶N O U N R
- V E B
- E C
- R T
- ⁷B I N T E R J E C T I O N
- O
- N

ACROSS

3. A word that takes the place of a noun.

4. A word that decorates a noun or a pronoun.

6. A word for a person, place, thing or idea.

7. A word or phrase that expresses surprise or emotion.

DOWN

1. A joining word that connects words or phrases.

2. A word that connects a noun or a pronoun to other words in a sentence.

4. A word that decorates a verb.

5. A word that shows an action or a state-of-being.

Student Page 168 – Lesson 28

The Three Goats Named Bruse
Final Draft

Write your final draft. Now you may add some creative touches. Keep the basic story and events, but make it your very own story by adding some adjectives and adverbs. You could add some detail about the poor food available in the goats' first pasture. You could add some more words to describe the Troll. How did the first goat feel when he first heard the Troll? The second? The third? What else could you add to the story?

Edit your writing using the following checklist:

1. Spelling – all the words are spelled correctly.

2. Sentences –

   Each sentence expresses a complete thought.

   Each one has a subject and a verb.

3. Capitalization –

   All the important words in the title begin with capital letters.

   Every sentence begins with a capital letter.

   The word "I" is capitalized, if used.

   All proper names start with capital letters.

4. Punctuation –

   All of your sentences end with periods or exclamation marks.

   Any questions end with question marks.

5. Quotes –

   You have included two or more direct quotes.

   You used quotation marks around the words spoken.

   You started a new line whenever a different character spoke.

6. Descriptions –

   Describe where your story takes place.

   Describe what your characters look like.

   Describe what your characters feel.

   Use adverbs to describe how your characters might have acted.

Show your finished story to your teacher or parent.

The Story of William Tell
by James Baldwin

The people of Switzerland were not always free and happy as they are today. Many years ago a proud tyrant, whose name was Gessler, ruled over them, and made their lot a bitter one indeed.

One day this tyrant set up a tall pole in the public square, and put his own cap on the top of it; and then he gave orders that every man who came into the town should bow down before it. But there was one man, named William Tell, who would not do this. He stood up straight with folded arms, and laughed at the swinging cap. He would not bow down to Gessler himself.

When Gessler heard of this, he was very angry. He was afraid that other men would disobey, and that soon the whole country would rebel against him. So he made up his mind to punish the bold man.

William Tell's home was among the mountains, and he was a famous hunter. No one in all the land could shoot with bow and arrow so well as he. Gessler knew this, and so he thought of a cruel plan to make the hunter's own skill bring him to grief. He ordered that Tell's little boy should be made to stand up in the public square with an apple on his head; and then he bade Tell shoot the apple with one of his arrows.

Tell begged the tyrant not to have him make this test of skill. What if the boy should move? What if the bowman's hand should tremble? What if the arrow should not carry true? "Will you make me kill my boy?" he said.

The Three Goats Named Bruse
Grammar Review

"Three **goats** once **lived** together on a mountain, and every one of **them** was named Bruse. It was hard for them to find enough to eat, for there were no trees there, **and** only a **few** blades of grass grew among the cracks and crevices of the rocks."

Circle the correct parts of speech:

1. goats   pronoun   interjection   (noun)

2. lived   noun   (verb)

3. them   (pronoun)   adjective   verb

4. and   pronoun   (conjunction)   adjective

5. few   conjunction   adverb   (adjective)

Why is the word *Bruse* capitalized? ___*Bruse* **is capitalized**___

___**because it is the goats' name.**___

Why is the word *It* capitalized? ___*It* **is capitalized**___

___**because it is the first word of a sentence.**___

167

Answer Key

The Story of William Tell
Copywork

Copy the following sentences from our story. Make sure your sentences have correct capitals and punctuation.

Then, without another word, Tell fitted the arrow to his bow. He took aim, and let it fly. The boy stood firm and still. He was not afraid, for he had all faith in his father's skill.

Check that the student has copied the passage

correctly. Check spelling, capital letters

and punctuation.

"Say no more," said Gessler. "You must hit the apple with your one arrow. If you fail, my soldiers shall kill the boy before your eyes."

Then, without another word, Tell fitted the arrow to his bow. He took aim, and let it fly. The boy stood firm and still. He was not afraid, for he had all faith in his father's skill.

The arrow whistled through the air. It struck the apple fairly in the center, and carried it away. The people who saw it shouted with joy.

As Tell was turning away from the place, an arrow which he had hidden under his coat dropped to the ground. "Fellow!" cried Gessler, "What mean you with this second arrow?"

"Tyrant!" was Tell's proud answer, "This arrow was for your heart if I had hurt my child."

And there is an old story, that, not long after this, Tell did shoot the tyrant with one of his arrows; and thus he set his country free.

The Story of William Tell
Quotation Review

Label each quote as Direct (D) or Indirect (I). If it is a direct quote, find and circle the quotation marks.

1. __I__ He bade Tell shoot the apple with one of his arrows.

2. __D__ "Will you make me kill my boy?" he said.

3. __D__ "Say no more," said Gessler.

Change the following quote from Direct to Indirect:

4. "Fellow!" cried Gessler, "What mean you with this second arrow?"

Gessler asked what Tell meant to do with the second arrow.

Change the following quote from Indirect to Direct:

5. He gave orders that every man who came into the town should bow down before it.

"Every man that comes into town shall bow down before it,"

he ordered.

The Story of William Tell
Vocabulary

Look up the following words and write down the meanings.
Write a short sentence using one of the words.

1. tyrant – **an absolute ruler, usually oppressive or**

harsh

2. bold – **daring; fearless**

3. skill – **great ability or proficiency**

Sentence: _____

169   Answer Key

The Story of William Tell
Spelling Practice

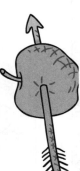

Make a spelling list of up to five words you misspelled and had to correct in your original rough draft. Write each word correctly two times.

1. _____   _____

2. _____   _____

ANSWERS WILL VARY

3. _____   _____

4. _____   _____

5. _____   _____

Now choose one of the words and use it in a sentence:

_____

_____

The Story of William Tell
Writing the Rough Draft

Read the story again. Write your rough draft of "William Tell." Don't forget to write about Tell refusing to bow before the cap on top of the pole. This made cruel Gessler very angry and determined to punish Tell. Was Tell's son afraid when he stood there with the apple on his head, or did he have faith in his father's skill with an arrow? Help your reader feel the thrill of the moment when the second arrow fell out of Tell's coat. When you are finished, read each sentence out loud to make sure it is a complete thought.

Edit your writing using the following checklist:

1. Spelling – all the words are spelled correctly. ___
2. Sentences –
   Each sentence expresses a complete thought. ___
   Each one has a subject and a verb. ___
3. Capitalization –
   All the important words in the title begin with capital letters. ___
   Every sentence begins with a capital letter. ___
   The word "I" is capitalized, if used. ___
   All proper names start with capital letters. ___
4. Punctuation –
   All of your sentences end with periods or exclamation marks. ___
   Any questions end with question marks. ___
5. Quotes –
   You have included two or more direct quotes. ___
   You used quotation marks around the words spoken. ___
   You started a new line whenever a different character spoke. ___
6. Descriptions –
   Describe where your story takes place. ___
   Describe what your characters look like. ___
   Describe what your characters feel. ___
   Use adverbs to describe how your characters might have acted. ___

6. Circle all the prepositions in the following sentence:

He ordered that Tell's little boy should be made to stand up (in) the public square (with) an apple (on) his head; and then he bade Tell shoot the apple (with) one (of) his arrows.

7. Circle all the conjunctions in the following sentences:

He took aim, (and) let it fly. The boy stood firm (and) still.

8. Circle the interjection in the following sentence:

"(Tyrant!)" was Tell's proud answer, "This arrow was for your heart if I had hurt my child."

The Story of William Tell
Grammar Review

1. Circle all the nouns in the following sentence: Many (years) ago a proud (tyrant,) whose (name) was (Gessler,) ruled over them, and made their (lot) bitter indeed.

2. Circle all the pronouns in the following sentence: One day this tyrant set up a tall pole in the public square, and put (his) own cap on the top of (it;) and then (he) gave orders that every man who came into the town should bow down before (it.)

3. Circle all the verbs in the following sentence: He (stood) up straight with folded arms, and (laughed) at the swinging cap.

4. Circle the adverb in the following sentence: When Gessler (finally) heard of this, he was angry.

5. Circle all the adjectives in the following sentence: Gessler knew this, and so he thought of a (cruel) plan to bring Tell to (great) grief.

Answer Key

The Story of William Tell
Final Draft

Write your final draft and add some creative touches. This is a historical story, so we need to keep the basic story and events, but make it your very own by adding details. Some suggestions: you could add more to the part where Tell refuses to bow to the hat. Add a direct quote from William Tell about how silly the hat looks. Add a direct quote from *Gessler* when he heard that Tell laughed at his hat. Tell your reader a little bit about why Tell was such a famous hunter. How about Tell's son? How did he react when he heard what he was going to have to do? Use adjectives and adverbs to add detail and interest to the events. It's up to you!

Edit your writing using the following checklist:

1. Spelling – all the words are spelled correctly. ___

2. Sentences –

   Each sentence expresses a complete thought. ___

   Each one has a subject and a verb. ___

3. Capitalization –

   All the important words in the title begin with
   capital letters. ___

   Every sentence begins with a capital letter. ___

   The word "I" is capitalized, if used. ___

   All proper names start with capital letters. ___

4. Punctuation –

   All of your sentences end with periods or
   exclamation marks. ___

   Any questions end with question marks. ___

5. Quotes –

   You have included two or more direct quotes. ___

   You used quotation marks around the words spoken. ___

   You started a new line whenever a different character spoke. ___

6. Descriptions –

   Describe where your story takes place. ___

   Describe what your characters look like. ___

   Describe what your characters feel. ___

   Use adverbs to describe how your characters might have acted. ___

Show your finished story to your teacher or parent.

Appendix A
Teaching Resources

Copy this page and cut apart the sentences so the students can practice putting the events of the story in order.

A Crow came upon a Pitcher which had once been full of water.

The Crow could not reach the little bit of water in the bottom of the Pitcher.

The Crow took a pebble and dropped it into the Pitcher.

Then the Crow took another pebble and dropped that into the Pitcher.

At last the Crow saw the water mount up near him.

The Crow was able to quench his thirst and save his life.

A Town Mouse went to visit his cousin in the country.

The Town Mouse did not like the country food.

"Come visit me," said the Town Mouse.

The two mice traveled to the town.

The two mice feasted on jellies and cakes.

The two mice heard dogs barking.

The Country Mouse ran home.

Androcles the slave escaped from his master.

Androcles came upon a Lion moaning and groaning.

The Lion's paw was swollen and bleeding.

Androcles pulled out the Lion's thorn.

The Lion took Androcles to his cave and fed him.

Androcles and the Lion were captured.

The Lion was very hungry.

Androcles was let loose in the arena for the Lion to eat.

The Emperor and his court came to watch.

The Lion licked Androcles hands.

Androcles and the Lion were freed by the Emperor.

Julius Caesar made himself ruler of Rome.

Caesar passed through a little country village.

Caesar's officers laughed at the village mayor.

Caesar said, "I would rather be the head man of a village than the second man in Rome!"

Caesar was crossing a narrow sea in a boat.

A storm overtook and threatened to sink Caesar's boat.

The captain was in a great fright.

Caesar was not afraid.

Caesar said, "The boat will not be lost; for you have Caesar on board."

The prince wanted to marry a princess, but he couldn't find a real one.

In the middle of a rainstorm a princess knocked on the door.

She said she was a real princess.

The old queen made her bed with twenty mattresses and one pea underneath them all.

The princess slept on the bed all night.

She said she slept very badly because the bed was uncomfortable.

They knew she was a real princess.

Kaboom

Kaboom

Kaboom

Kaboom

Kaboom

Wow!

Go jump in the lake.

I like purple and yellow flowers.

Do you like blue pickles?

The dog ran away.

Our house is small.

Melissa ate four cookies last night.

The basketball team won three games last week.

Why is the sky blue?

Should Kristen go walk the dog?

Don't tell anyone.

Why did the lion's paw hurt him?

Eat your dinner.

Eat your turnips before your chocolate cake.

Shall we go out for ice cream?

Kristen won the game!

I like to make milkshakes for dinner.

The Town Mouse ran around the house.

I love mowing the lawn!

I love mushrooms!

Timothy played baseball yesterday.

Yay for our team!

Stop teasing your sister.

This bread is stale!

Water the garden now.

How many brownies would you like?

Go jump on the trampoline.

Sentence Strips for "Ka-Boom", Lesson 9, Set 2 – Direct vs. Indirect Quotes

Kaboom

Kaboom

Kaboom

Kaboom

Kaboom

The Crow said, "I think I'll drop some pebbles into the water pitcher."

The Crow told his friends how he was able to get a drink.

The Town Mouse said, "Of course you cannot expect anything better in the country."

The Town Mouse offered his cousin some refreshment.

The Country Mouse nervously asked about the growling and barking outside the door.

"It is only the dogs of the house," said the Town Mouse.

"Good-bye, Cousin!" said the Country Mouse.

Androcles said to the Lion, "Give me your paw."

Androcles was told he would be thrown to the lions.

Androcles told the Emperor about his friend, the Lion.

"You may go free," said the Emperor.

"I am now ruler of Rome," announced Julius Caesar.

Some said that Caesar wished to become king.

The mayor told the people to stand by the road and watch Caesar pass.

"See how that fellow struts at the head of his little flock!" said the army officer to Caesar.

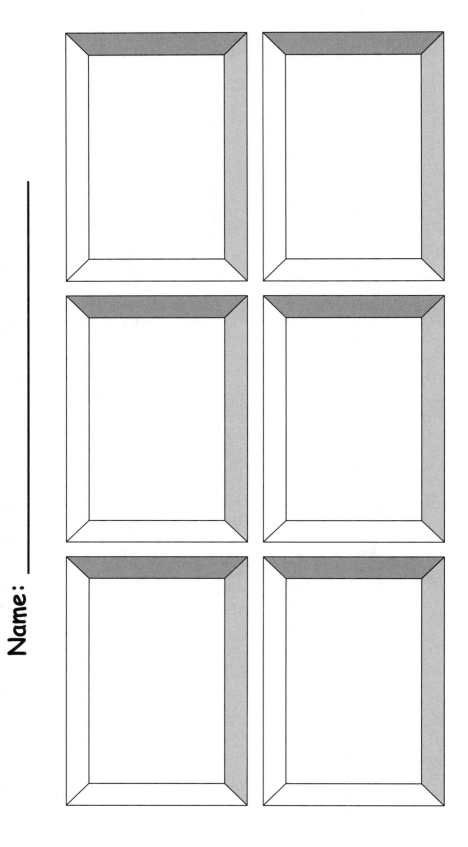

Storyboard

Title: _____

Name: _____

Name That Noun

Person

Place

_____

_____

_____

_____

_____

_____

_____

_____

_____

_____

_____

_____

_____

_____

Thing

Idea

_____

_____

_____

_____

_____

_____

_____

_____

_____

_____

_____

_____

_____

_____

Appendix

Word Cards for "ID Tic Tac Toe"; Lesson 13; Noun and Pronouns

tree	bird	cat	monkey
hearth	story	bench	shoemaker
Emperor	lion	cat	monkey
village	road	country	king
hut	sword	peace	idea
chestnut	joy	you	he
him	our	mine	them
it	they	we	I

The King declared that the first man to beat his daughter in a race may have her for a wife.

Many men tried to race the princess and lost.

A poor young man challenged the princess to a race.

The young man dropped roses at the princess' feet.

The princess picked up the roses and smelled them.

The young man dropped a silken girdle.

The princess buckled the beautiful girdle about her waist.

The young man dropped a silken bag with a golden ball in it.

The princess paused to play with the golden ball.

The young man won the race.

Action Verbs: Active Anna
Story and artwork created by Katrina Bender

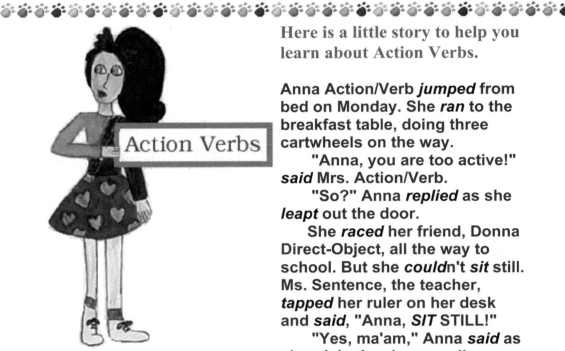

Here is a little story to help you learn about Action Verbs.

Anna Action/Verb *jumped* from bed on Monday. She *ran* to the breakfast table, doing three cartwheels on the way.

"Anna, you are too active!" *said* Mrs. Action/Verb.

"So?" Anna *replied* as she *leapt* out the door.

She *raced* her friend, Donna Direct-Object, all the way to school. But she *could*n't *sit* still. Ms. Sentence, the teacher, *tapped* her ruler on her desk and *said*, "Anna, *SIT* STILL!"

"Yes, ma'am," Anna *said* as she *picked* up her pencil.

When the class *lined* up for Art, Patrick Pronoun *whispered*, "You'd better *stop* being so active. You'll *get* into trouble." But Anna *was seeing* how long she *could hop* on one foot and not *trip* over Donna.

The Art teacher, Mrs. Preposition, *was showing* the class how to draw snowflakes when Anna *tipped* over in her chair. Then she *did* five somersaults right into a table. Anna *got* a bruise on her forehead and *had* to go to the nurse.

Then Mr. Noun, the principal, *wrote* a note home to Anna's parents. And can you *guess* what Mr. and Mrs. Action/Verb *decided*? No gymnastics, Anna's favorite class, for a week!

So Anna *learned* to do flips only in gymnastics and to learn in school instead.

You should have learned in this story that action verbs are used to show when somebody does something. Action verbs in this story are in *italics*.

State-of-Being Verbs

Story created by Lisa Farnell, artwork created by Katrina Bender

Here is a little story to help you learn about the <u>eight</u> state-of-being verbs:

Once upon a time there *was* a nice boy named Stately. He *was* very prim and proper. Stately *was* an A+ student. One day at school, there *was* going to be a big test on verbs. Stately knew all the action verbs but he didn't want to forget the eight state-of-being verbs. He needed a way to remember them so he could get an A+ on the big test. As he sat there thinking of ideas, he found himself humming a rhythm, "Da, da, da-da, da, da, da, da. All of a sudden he jumped up and shouted, "That *is* it! That *is* the rhythm I need to remember the state-of-being verbs: *Is, am, were, was, are, be, being, been.*"

The next day, he went to school humming and clapping the rhythm the whole way. When he got his graded test back he had earned an A+, and Stately was very happy. After he got the A+ he changed his name to Stately State-of-Being Verb because he just *IS* so stately.

> You should have learned in this story that state-of-being verbs are verbs that state that something IS.

Reprinted with permission from the Kyrene de las Brisas Elementary School Website.

Appendix

Two young boys watched a mother and a friend walk among the flowers and the trees.

The boys decided that their mother looked like a queen.

The mother invited her boys to share lunch with her and her friend.

The mother's friend showed them a magnificent casket of jewels.

The mother's friend asked Cornelia if she was poor.

Cornelia told her friend that her boys were her jewels.

197

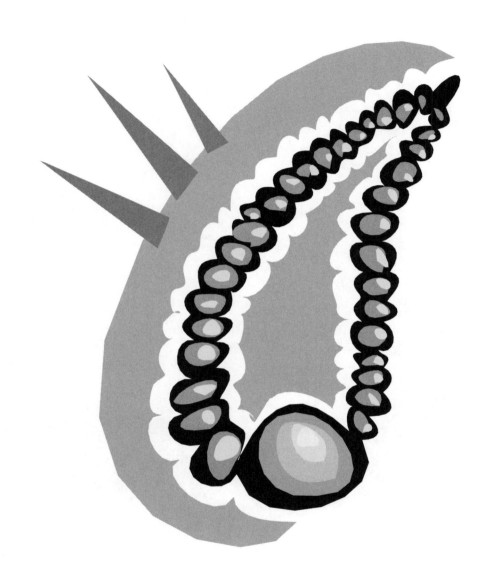

Word Cards for "ID Tic Tac Toe"; Lesson 18; Verbs and Adjectives

run	walk	crawl	chew
read	write	talk	drive
eat	is	was	are
be	being	were	jump
pretty	delicious	red	new
bright	dull	exciting	boring
sad	quick	old	shiny
slippery	slimy	sharp	heavy

scornfully	gently	bravely	rarely
equally	safely	tenderly	usually
daily	never	always	inside
outside	tomorrow	then	quickly

above	across	after	around
at	before	behind	below
beside	between	by	down
during	for	from	into

King Alfred and the Cakes
Fun with Parts of Speech

Ask the students for the various kinds of words without revealing the story, then read the finished product out loud.

Many years ago there lived in England a _____ (adj.) and _____ (adj.) _____ (noun, person) whose name was Alfred. Between _____ (verb) and _____ (verb) he had a busy time of it indeed. Alfred was very _____ (adj.) and _____ (adj.) and as he _____ (verb) in the _____ (noun, place), he _____ (adv.) begged a woman to give him something to eat and a place to sleep in her _____ (noun). The woman was baking some _____ (noun pl.) on her hearth, and she looked with pity upon the poor, _____ (adj.) fellow who seemed so hungry. "Yes," she said, "I will give you some supper if you will watch these _____ (same noun as last one). I want to go out and _____ (verb) the _____ (noun); and you must see that they do not burn while I am gone."

Alfred was very willing to do this, but he had far _____ (adj.) things to think about. He forgot his job for his mind was busy. In a little while the woman came back _____ (adv.). The supper was smoking on the hearth, burned _____ (adv.) to a crisp. Ah, how _____ (adv.) angry she was! "You _____ (adj.) fellow!" she cried. "See what you have done! You want something to eat, but you do not want to _____ (verb)!"

A dollmaker in China made a little doll.

A little girl saw Ching in a toy shop and wanted him.

A rich tea merchant sent Ching to America.

A rich little girl did not want Ching.

Ching sat for a long time in a flower bed.

An old gentleman gave Ching to his cook.

The cook did not want clutter in her kitchen and threw Ching into the rubbish can.

The rubbish man sold Ching for fifteen cents.

The laundry man cleaned Ching and mailed him to China.

The little girl who loved Ching got him for her own.

<u>Silly Sentence Activity for Lesson 24; Learning Conjunctions</u>

Make as many sentences as you can by combining one word or phrase from each column.

The dollmaker made Ching	because	she had too many toys.
The little girl did not want Ching	however	he glued him with the best glue.
	after	
Ching tumbled down		he fell into the flower bed.
	until	
A laundry man bought him		he washed and cleaned Ching.
	but	
Ching went on a long journey		he needed to find a home.

and	but	or	however
therefore	wow	cool	unreal
hey	no	hmmm	whoops
oh	ah	alas	ouch

Appendix B
Supplemental Texts

Fables by Arnold Lobel, HarperTrophy, 1980.

Punctuation Takes a Vacation by Robin Pulver, Holiday House, 2003.

Squids Will Be Squids: Fresh Morals, Beastly Fables by Jon Scieszka, Penguin Putnam Books for Young Readers, 1998.

Where the Sidewalk Ends, by Shel Silverstein, HarperCollins, 1974.

Fantastic! Wow! And Unreal! A Book about Interjections and Conjunctions, by Ruth Heller, Puffin Books, 1998.

Appendix C
Game Synopses

KA-BOOM

Introduced in Lesson 5.

Set-up: Copy the "Ka-Boom" pages from Appendix A. You may wish to copy them on cardstock for durability. For additional durability, I recommend "laminating" them with clear shelf paper. Put the strips in an empty, clean potato chip can. Paste a piece of colorful paper around the barrel of the can and write "Ka-boom!" on it.

Play: Students draw strips out of the can one at a time and tell you what kind of sentence it is.* If they are correct, they keep the sentence strip. If incorrect, they must put it back in the can. If they draw "Ka-boom!" they must put all of their strips back in the can. The student with the most strips at the end of the game wins. If you are playing with just one student, you may choose an amount of time to play the game and see how many strips the child has at the end of the time. Perhaps you could trade chocolate candies, peanuts or raisins – one or two for each sentence strip the child still has at the end!

*Variation introduced in Lesson 8: Indicate a punctuation mark on the sentence that the student has chosen and ask for the "movement" that the "traffic signal" tells; i.e., stop, pause, stop and then move on.

** Variation introduced in Lesson 9: Use the "Simple Quotes" sentence strips from Appendix A. The student will tell you whether the sentence contains a direct quote or an indirect quote.

*** Variation introduced in Lesson 10: Have the student change a direct quote to an indirect quote, and vice versa.

Red Light, Green Light

Introduced in Lesson 7.

This game works best with three or more players, but may be adapted to be played with only two (teacher and student) as well.

One player is the Traffic Cop and stands at one end of the room. The other players line up at the other end. The Traffic Cop calls out "Capital Letter!" (instead of "Green Light") when he wants the other players to start moving. The other players walk towards the Traffic Cop. The Traffic Cop can call out "Exclamation Point!" or "Period!" or "Question Mark!" when he wants the other players to stop. He may then start them up again by calling "Capital Letter!" The Traffic Cop may also call out, "Comma!" at which point the students must stop, say "Take a break!" and then continue on. If the Traffic Cop catches anyone not following his instructions, he may send them back to start. The first student to reach the Traffic Cop becomes the next Traffic Cop.

Name That Noun

Introduced in Lesson 11.

Homeschool Directions: Copy and hand out the game page from Appendix A. Play with one column at a time. The first round will be "Persons". You will each have two minutes to write down as many nouns for "persons" that you can think of. You may either play to see how many each of you can come up with, or you may compare your lists, cross out the duplicates, and only score points for the original nouns. Play again with "Places," "Things," and "Ideas."

Co-op Directions: Copy and hand out the game page from Appendix A. Play with one column at a time. The first round will be "Persons". Give the students two minutes to write down as many nouns for "persons" that they can think of. You may either play to see how many each student can come up with, or have the students compare their lists, cross out the duplicates, and only score points for the original nouns. Play again with "Places," "Things," and "Ideas."

ID Tic Tac Toe

Introduced in Lesson 13.

Copy the word page (Nouns and Pronouns) from Appendix A onto stiff card stock, cut into word squares and put into a bag. Divide students into two teams: Xs and Os. Alternate turns between the players of the two teams. On his turn, the player will pull one word square from the bag and must identify it as either a noun or a pronoun. If he is correct, he may place an X or an O for his team onto a tic tac toe board. If he is incorrect, he forfeits his turn.

In Lesson 18, add the Verb and Adjective word cards.

In Lesson 21, add the Adverb and Preposition word cards.

In Lesson 25, add the Conjunction and Interjection word cards.

Verb Charades

Introduced in Lesson 15.

Together brainstorm as many action verbs as possible for three minutes. Write the action verbs on the board or on a piece of paper. Then illustrate that these verbs show action by playing charades. One student secretly chooses an action verb from the board, and then acts it out while the other students guess which one it is. The student who guesses correctly goes next.

Grammar Tic-Tac-Toe

Introduced in Lesson 16.

Divide the students into two teams, or play with your student. Alternating teams, each player must give the grammar definition you ask for correctly before placing an X or O on the board. If they are wrong, play forfeits to the other team. Ask the part-of-speech definitions that you have already learned, using noun, pronoun, verb, adjective, adverb, preposition, conjunction, or interjection.

The Necklace Game

Introduced in Lesson 17.

Homeschool Directions: Use the five pictures of necklaces from Appendix A. Ask your student to secretly choose one of the necklace pictures, and then describe it to you using only adjectives. Your job is to guess which necklace he is describing. Repeat as time allows.

Co-op Directions: Use the five pictures of necklaces from Appendix A. Call one or two students up and secretly show them one necklace picture. Then ask them to describe to the rest of the class their necklace, using only adjectives. The other students will guess which necklace they are describing. Repeat with the other students.

Jumping Interjections

Introduced in Lesson 25.

Homeschool Directions: Toss a ball back and forth to each other, saying an interjection each time you pass the ball. The object is not to get stuck for an interjection and not to repeat an interjection that has already been used.

Co-op Directions: Stand with the students in a circle. Pass the ball to a student across from you while saying an interjection. That student will pass the ball to another student while saying another interjection. See how long you can go without repeating interjections or getting stuck for one. *Optional:* If a student can't come up with one or repeats one, he must sit down. Play until you have a winner.